BEATLES
MEMORABILIA

THE **JULIAN LENNON** COLLECTION

GIBSON LES PAUL JUNIOR

This guitar was a gift from John Lennon
to his son Julian in 1973. For more
information, see pages 146–7.

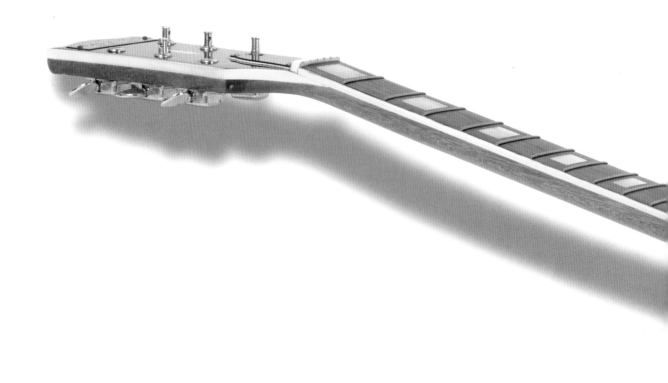

THIS IS A CARLTON BOOK

Published in 2010 by Goodman Books
An imprint of the Carlton Publishing Group
20 Mortimer Street
London W1T 3JW

Memorabilia and foreword © 2010 Lennon by Lennon
Design and text copyright © 2010 Carlton Books Limited

A CIP catalogue record for this book is available from the British Library.

ISBN 978-1-84796-018-4

Book design and layout: Peter Dawson, www.gradedesign.com

Printed in Dubai

BEATLES
MEMORABILIA

THE **JULIAN LENNON** COLLECTION

BRIAN SOUTHALL WITH JULIAN LENNON

GOODMAN

CONTENTS

THIS BOOK IS DEDICATED TO THE FOUR LADS
FROM LIVERPOOL WHO CHANGED THE WORLD ...
AND TO ALL THEIR FANS WHO KEEP THEIR MUSIC ALIVE NOW AND FOREVER ...
AND TO MY MOTHER, CYNTHIA.

FOREWORD

I realized recently that I've been collecting Beatles memorabilia for nearly 20 years. Amazing! Every item means something to me but it is the collection as a whole which is most important and special. For me the collection represents my life, my history, my heritage, so it's wonderful that I now have the chance to share my collection and my memories with you in this unique book, the first time my Beatles memorabilia collection has been featured in print.

When I started collecting I only had a couple of items, including the two guitars Dad had given me. When he passed away in 1980 I didn't inherit any mementoes or keepsakes, which was incredibly sad for me and my family. Nearly everything I now own I had to buy at auction, so I'm especially grateful and touched that friends like Paul McCartney and May Pang have occasionally given me something that Dad once owned.

I have never had any specific masterplan in mind for the collection, I just go with my heart. If I hear of something which stirs a certain memory of a particular time or place then I go for it. Unfortunately, I haven't always managed to get what I've bid on at auction. Beatles memorabilia is highly collectible and the demand for it is very competitive. But what's nice is that on the odd occasion – although I buy anonymously – if rival bidders have discovered it's me, they've dropped out and let me have the item. Many people, like me, believe that these possessions should be with me and the Liverpool Lennon family; it's our history. I think of the collection as organic – it's not complete and I'll add to it as and when the right thing comes along.

All the pieces I have collected have their own special memories and stories but some are particular favourites. One of my most treasured pieces is the Monkey Bike. I have such great memories of riding around on it as a small kid with Dad, and it's certainly where my love of motorbikes began. Despite Dad being the worst driver ever he certainly had a few unforgettable cars, like the psychedelic Rolls-Royce and the Austin Maxi he crashed in Scotland in 1969 with me in it! I also remember Dad's old stretch Mercedes which had a sideways record player in the back – I'd love to find out what happened to that.

Until recently almost all the memorabilia was kept in storage but it occurred to me how pointless it was keeping everything locked up. I started wondering whether people would be interested in seeing the collection and with that in mind we created the travelling exhibition, 'White Feather: The Spirit of Lennon'. I'm very proud of the exhibition and I'm pleased that its success has allowed a share of the proceeds from it – and from this book – to go to my charity.

This book has been great fun to put together and I love seeing the collection in print. I hope you do too!

Peace and love and respect,

Julian Lennon

Julian Lennon, 2010

INTRODUCTION

Part of the research for this book involved me taking two trips. One to a historic city with a wealth of musical heritage and one to see the person whose commitment to ensuring that the memory of a true icon of popular music should continue to be celebrated (and not mourned), which also led to the creation of this work.

Liverpool, for those of us of a certain age who grew up in the 1960s, remains very much the focal point of Britain's rock 'n' pop heritage. Going back there after more than a decade still brought back memories of the era of Mersey Beat, which so dominated my life as a teenager. Walking round the city's 'White Feather: The Spirit of John Lennon' exhibition served only to stir more thoughts of an extraordinary time when the antics and achievements of four young men from Liverpool made headline news.

Travelling further afield to see Julian, the son of John Lennon, was a unique opportunity to swap tales about the music industry – which has engaged both of us for most of our adult lives – and more importantly to understand his passion behind the collecting of memorabilia covering the life of his late father.

Throughout our conversation Julian talked proudly and candidly about his father – the man whose job as one of the most famous people on the planet took him away from his first-born son for weeks and months at a time – and also about the items which occupy a special place in the memories of his childhood years.

At the same time I was able to throw his way some stories from my 15-year career with The Beatles' record company, EMI. Although John Lennon was the only Beatle I never met – and the one I wanted to meet most of all – I did work on his various solo releases during the 1970s and was constantly entertained by the witty and at times cruelly sarcastic telexes and postcards he sent to the company on a regular basis from his new home in New York.

His impact on the great British company, and the people who worked there, lived on during my time and those who were there during the hectic and unforgettable days of Beatlemania talked of his creativity, stubbornness, excess, wit, curiosity, passion – and unending suspicion of big business.

In an effort to give all of us fans of the 'fab four' – both collectively and individually – a further insight into the personality of John Lennon, his son has created a unique tribute to his father which celebrates a life that ended all too soon.

When Julian was born in 1963, The Beatles were on the verge of becoming a global phenomenon and even with the best will in the world, there wasn't much room for family life in a hectic pop schedule built around performing, touring, promoting and recording.

As he grew up, Julian came to realize that family life for the Lennons was never going to be normal. "Growing up as John Lennon's son has been a rocky path," is how he sums it all up as he looks back on a childhood spent greedily savouring every moment he got to be with his dad: "He was a great talent, a remarkable man who stood for love and peace in the world, but to me he was the father I loved and longed for in his many absences."

And to make things more difficult, not only was his dad famous, but he also had some pretty well-known mates who played in the same band. "Dad was only a little further ahead in being a friend or a parent than the others," says Julian today. "Paul was very caring and very attentive, and George and I had a lovely bond. In many respects on a personal level they were all sort of uncles to me."

That closeness, coupled with his own genuine feeling of gratitude for the love and care they showed toward him, is at the heart of his collection of memorabilia and memories which are displayed and chronicled in this book.

When he decided to forge his own career in music, Julian always knew and understood that it would be a difficult path to follow his father's extraordinary and unique achievements both as a member of the all-conquering Beatles and as a solo artist.

"Never mind being the son of… or the association with The Beatles, it's hard enough trying to be a songwriter anyway. You are dealing with three incredibly talented songwriters and then to be compared to them as a single solo artist is slightly unfair," is his own assessment of the situation he found himself in.

As he says, "the Beatles were a tough act to follow" but follow them he did and in 1984 he achieved global success with his debut album *Valotte* and notched up two top-ten singles with the title track and 'Too Late For Goodbyes'. Four more albums followed – *The Secret Value of Daydreaming*, *Mr Jordan*, *Help Yourself* and the critically acclaimed *Photograph Smile* – which again brought him chart success worldwide.

Now, while he continues to commit his time to his White Feather Foundation and to ensuring his father's life and works are properly remembered and recognized, Julian has also returned to the recording studio. "I finished my new album two years ago and waited to see which way the music industry was going to go before deciding when to release it," he says, happy that he has found his own "real style" on his new album.

Even so, there is no denying that his father and his playmates – Paul, George and Ringo – have influenced Julian. "The Beatles' music has been an incredible influence to me as a person and as a songwriter. I always looked up to them – The Beatles and not necessarily just Dad – as having a great formula for songwriting. Everything they did, how they structured songs and put them together, was amazing stuff."

This book is testimony to Julian Lennon's determination to bring together pieces of The Beatles' story and his own father's life, which are first and foremost of importance to him and his family, but also part of all our lives as fans of the most successful and most influential artists of the twentieth century.

Read on, enjoy, and while you're at it, why not – in the words of the late great, John L – give peace a chance?

Brian Southall, 2010

THERE'S A PLACE

THE BUSTLING PORT OF LIVERPOOL IN THE LATE 1950S WAS THE BIRTHPLACE OF THE QUARRYMEN, JOHNNY AND THE MOONDOGS AND THE SILVER BEATLES BEFORE FOUR TEENAGERS – MAD FOR THE EXCITING SOUL, ROCK AND POP MUSIC THEY HEARD OVER THE AIRWAVES AND ON THE LOCAL JUKEBOXES AS IT SWEPT IN FROM AMERICA – GAVE THEMSELVES A NEW IDENTITY AND SET ABOUT PUTTING THE BEATLES ON THE MAP.

HOFNER CLUB 50 GUITAR

This is one of a series of guitars launched in the late 1950s by the German instrument company Hofner, who created their first guitars around 1920. It is one of the 1958 series and most likely used by John during the period when he was in The Silver Beatles, and the first years of The Beatles. Julian was given the guitar as a gift after his father's death.

The earliest Hofner 50 models had the oval-shaped four tone and volume console while later versions boasted a rectangular console. It ran alongside the Club 40, 60 and & 70 series and Hofner later issued a limited edition Club 40 based on one owned by John Lennon when he was in The Quarrymen, which was bought for him by his aunt Mimi on instalments for more than £30.

Hofner guitars were also among the earliest guitars bought and used by both Paul McCartney and George Harrison in the early days of The Beatles. Paul first saw a violin-shaped Hofner bass in Hamburg during the group's visits to the Kaiserkeller and Indra clubs, and paid the equivalent of about £30 for the "lovely instrument" which, according to him, "became a kind of trademark."

George's second guitar was the acoustic Hofner President, which he described as "quite nice," but eventually swapped with one of the Swinging Blue Jeans for his third guitar – a Hofner Club 40.

EARLY PHOTOGRAPHS

The three 'live' photographs of John Lennon in his late teens or early 20s were taken by local Liverpool musician Pete Best at the Casbah Club in West Derby, which was opened and run by his mother. John has switched from his American rock 'n' roll Elvis-inspired quiff and 'DA' (duck's arse) hairstyle to a shorter cut.

The single shot of John from around the same era was taken at Paul's home at Forthlin Road in the Allerton district of Liverpool. It was here that John and Paul first wrote together, often while playing truant from school, and songs like 'Just Fun', 'One After 909' and even an early version of 'Love Me Do' – which were listed by Paul in a school exercisebook under the heading 'Another Lennon/McCartney original' – were all composed in the three bed-roomed terraced council house where Paul's father Jim also allowed

The Quarrymen to rehearse.

Best's mother Mona opened the Casbah Club in the cellar of her large Victorian house in the West Derby district of Liverpool on August 29, 1959 and The Quarrymen – Lennon, McCartney, Harrison and Kenny Brown – were the first resident group and played seven shows there on Saturday nights from September to October 1959.

By the time they returned to play two dates at the Casbah in December 1960, the band had been renamed The Beatals (briefly) and then the Silver Beatles before becoming simply The Beatles. They had earlier lost guitarist Brown and recruited bassist Stuart Sutcliffe although he was briefly replaced by Chas Newby for four dates in December 1960 – including the Casbah shows – by Chas Newby.

The Beatles went on to play more than 30 shows at the Casbah between

1961 and their final appearance on June 24 1962 – just a week ahead of the club closing for the last time. The Casbah was not only important in the development of The Beatles as an early regular venue but also served as their 'office' from where Mrs Best and son Pete often helped organize the group's schedule. In December 1961 The Beatles – John, Paul, George and Pete, who by now was a member of the group – met Brian Epstein in the club to discuss the details of their new management contract.

Looking at these early photographs, Julian says:

"These pictures are from a time before it all went berserk for The Beatles. I like them because for me it's Dad at a time of innocence before it all went to pot, before it all went pear-shaped in both good and bad ways. They are very natural shots of a young man doing what he loved doing best – playing music.

"Strangely enough in the photos where he's playing live he reminds me of Peter Sellers, the look and the smile is remarkably like the early Sellers. Dad had a very specific stage look. He couldn't see, of course – he was as blind as a bat – and that's how his stage look developed ... head back, squinting. I was amazed when I heard that he couldn't actually see when he was on stage, and when he did, it scared the life out of him!"

1962 LIFE ASSURANCE POLICY// OPPOSITE

On November 20, 1962, just a month after his 22nd birthday, John took out a 25-year life policy with the giant Pearl Assurance company, which was established in a pub in the London district of Whitechapel in 1857.

It's quite possible he took it out in Liverpool during the day as The Beatles were scheduled to play at Southport that evening, having returned from a gig in Birmingham at the West Bromwich Adelphi the night before. The Beatles' first single 'Love Me Do', had come out six weeks earlier and recording for their first Parlophone album started on November 26, 1962, the day after the 25-year policy came into effect.

John, who was living with his aunt Mimi at Mendips at the time, seems to have decided to pay the annual premium of £10 18s 4d (approximately £10) in four quarterly instalments of £2.14s 7d.

PEARL
ASSURANCE COMPANY, LIMITED

CHIEF OFFICES: HIGH HOLBORN, LONDON, W.C.1.

(Incorporated in England under Act of Parliament 25th and 26th Victoria Cap. 89.)

Pearl Assurance Company Limited has its Registered Offices at High Holborn, London, W.C.1, to which address alone all Notices affecting this Policy must be sent.

Whereas the Proposer named in the Schedule set out below is desirous of effecting an Assurance with PEARL ASSURANCE COMPANY LIMITED (hereinafter called "the Company") and has signed and caused to be delivered to the Company a Proposal bearing the date mentioned in the Schedule hereto containing statements and particulars declared and warranted to be true and complete and expressing agreement that such statements and particulars shall be (and the same are hereby admitted to be) the basis of the contract between the Company and the Proposer.

Now this Policy Witnesseth that provided the Company receive the Premiums mentioned in the Schedule on the dates therein specified the Company will upon the happening of the event mentioned in the Schedule pay the Sum Assured mentioned in the said Schedule to the Proposer or the Executors Administrators or Assigns of the Proposer.

Provided always that the Schedule and all the Conditions endorsed hereon are to be deemed part of this Policy and of the contract made between the Company and the Proposer in the same manner as if the same were actually repeated herein.

SCHEDULE

Number of Policy		Date of Policy	Table	Agency Code
	2510081 A	27th November 1962	VIA	H.10/4
Name and Address of the Proposer	John Winston Lennon 251 Menlove Avenue, Liverpool 25			

			Whether age admitted
Name and Address of the life in respect whereof the Assurance is granted	As above		
	herein called "the Assured" and stated in the proposal to have been born on	9.10.1940	Not admitted

Date of Proposal	20th November 1962
Sum Assured	£ 1,000 (One Thousand Pounds) With Profits
Event or Events on which the Sum Assured is to become payable	The expiration of the full term of **twenty-five** years from the date hereof or the earlier death of the Assured.

Premium	Amount	Payable on the date hereof and thereafter quarterly in advance on 27th February May August and November	Period during which payable The whole duration of the Assurance.
	£ 10 : 18 : 4		

SPECIAL CONDITIONS

In the event of the sum assured becoming payable on the death of the Assured, such death having occurred before the attainment by the Assured of age 65 years and as a direct result of bodily injury caused by violent accidental external and visible means sustained within Great Britain, Ireland, the Isle of Man, the Channel Islands or the continent of Europe and within three calendar months of such accident and such death not having been occasioned or accelerated by self-injury or intemperance or by engaging in aviation (otherwise than as a fare-paying passenger during peacetime on a regular public air-line) and such death not directly or indirectly having arisen from or been caused by or been traceable to civil commotion or war or hostilities of any kind the Company will pay a further sum equal to the sum assured exclusive of any bonus additions thereto to the person or persons to whom the sum assured is expressed to be payable.

In Witness whereof this Policy has been signed on behalf and with the authority of the Company on the date of Policy mentioned in the above Schedule.

Examined

W Ewart Ford,
Director.

W. L. Grant,
General Manager.

AUTOGRAPHS

This signed pre-printed card includes the signature of the original Beatles' drummer Pete Best and came from a special one-off show at the famous Cavern Club in Matthew Street, Liverpool on April 5, 1962, which was presented by The Beatles fan club.

This show was billed as 'The Beatles For Their Fans – or 'An evening with George John, Paul & Pete' – and it also featured local DJ Bob Wooler (billed as "the Beatles favourite Compere") plus support act The Four Jays, who would later change their name to the Fourmost and become one of Brian Epstein's stable of Mersey Beat acts. Tickets for the 7.30pm show cost 6s/6d and included a free photograph of The Beatles.

Best was the drummer with local Liverpool group The Blackjacks when he was invited to audition for The Beatles in August 1960, and he made his debut with them in Germany in August 1960 when they played over 100 shows in Hamburg between August and November.

John's memory of hiring Best was very simple: "We knew of a guy and he had a drum kit, so we just grabbed him, auditioned him and he could keep one beat going for long enough so we took him."

For the next two years Best played with The Beatles throughout the northwest of England and also in Germany, and was drummer on the tape sent to EMI in 1961 and at the live audition for Decca on New Year's Day in 1962 when the Beatles were rejected by both companies.

His best friend was a young accountant named Neil Aspinall, who lodged with the Best family and had been to the Liverpool Institute with Paul and George. Eventually he became The Beatles 'roadie' and personal assistant before being named as managing director of their Apple Corps company, a position he held until his death in 2008.

By the time The Beatles arrived in London in June 1963 to audition for EMI at Abbey Road studios with Parlophone manager George Martin, Best's position within the Beatles was in jeopardy. On the occasions when he failed to turn up for gigs they had recruited a stand-in local drummer called Ringo Starr who, they all agreed, seemed to fit their music better.

It seems that George Martin was also less than sure of Best's suitability for the role as drummer with The Beatles and eventually he was sacked by Epstein on August 15, 1962, following a sell-out lunchtime gig with the group at the Cavern Club.

Epstein recalled that he was called by the other three Beatles and told, "We want Pete out and Ringo in." He added, "I decided that if the group was to remain, happy Pete Best must go and I knew that I would have to do it quickly and decisively." John later admitted: "We were cowards when we sacked him. We made Brian do it."

However, Best's firing was big news in Liverpool and in the weeks that followed his dismissal there was something of a revolt in Liverpool with fans chanting "Pete Best for ever – Ringo never!" while George Harrison

was assaulted and Epstein – who described himself at the time as the "most hated man in Liverpool" – was forced to hire a bodyguard for his visits to the Cavern.

The local *Mersey Beat* paper carried the story of The Beatles' changing drummer and printed the official line from the group, which read; "Pete left the group by mutual agreement. There were no arguments or difficulties and this has been an entirely amicable decision." At the same time Best gave the paper his version of events: "The news came as a big surprise to me as I had had no hint that it could happen and didn't even have the opportunity of discussing it with the rest of the group."

For his part, John took the view that a discussion would not have been the best way of dealing with the situation: "If we had told him to his face that would have been much nastier. It would probably have ended in a fight."

After The Beatles, life for Best involved joining rival Liverpool band Lee Curtis & the All Stars, getting married to his childhood sweetheart, forming the Pete Best Four and then the Pete Best Combo before eventually leaving the music business in the late 1960s and becoming a civil servant. Later he reformed the Pete Best Band – which still tours in America – and he received a substantial windfall in royalties in 1965 following the release of The Beatles' *Anthology 1* album, which contained around a dozen early recordings that he had made with The Beatles.

With Best Wishes

from

Paul   Pete

John   George

THE BEATLES

April 5th 1962

GIBSON SG
ELECTRIC GUITAR, 1959

This solid-bodied Gibson guitar was launched in late 1950s or early 1960s by the American guitar company which was founded in Nashville, Tennessee in 1902. It was a model once owned by John Lennon, which was also favoured by The Searchers' John McNally and by Eric Clapton during his time with Cream.

There has long been debate as to the actual meaning of the 'SG' with some claiming that it simply stands for 'solid guitar' while others believe it means 'Standard Gibson'. Although veteran guitarist Les Paul was never officially involved with the SG range of guitars, some models were made with a Les Paul nameplate in the neck.

FROM ME TO YOU

JOHN LENNON, PAUL MCCARTNEY, GEORGE HARRISON AND NEW BOY DRUMMER RINGO STARR, UNDER THE EVER-WATCHFUL EYE OF MANAGER BRIAN EPSTEIN, FOUND THEMSELVES AT THE FOREFRONT OF A BRITISH REVOLUTION IN THE EARLY 1960S. THE 'BEAT BOOM' TOOK OVER THE CHARTS, GROUPS REPLACED SINGERS AND THE BEATLES' OWN DISTINCT BRAND OF HOME-GROWN POP MUSIC TOOK THEM ON A UNIQUE AND EXTRAORDINARY JOURNEY TOWARD GLOBAL DOMINATION.

POINTS TO REMEMBER ▮▮▮▮▮▮▮▮▮

Give E.M.I. Record Tokens (6/- to 50/-) exchangeable for all leading makes of records ▮ For latest information on the 'POPS' read the Record Mail ▮ To take good care of this record—check your stylus regularly and use 'Emitex' cleaning material.

▮ THIS RECORD MUST BE PLAYED AT 45 R.P.M. ▮

E.M.I. RECORDS LTD • HAYES • MIDDLESEX • ENGLAND

Made and Printed in Great Britain

'SHE LOVES YOU' SAMPLE DISC

Released on August 23, 1963 as the fourth Beatles' single on EMI's Parlophone label with the number R5055, 'She Loves You' – and its B-side, 'I'll Get You' – was The Beatles' second British number one single. It held the top spot for four weeks before being dislodged for the next seven weeks and then eventually returned to the top for two more weeks.

The letter A sticker on this disc shows that it was an early sample copy, probably sent to radio stations or the press, and the sticker made it clear to producers, disc jockeys and reviewers which was the A-side of the record … and therefore the one they should play or review.

'She Loves You' was recorded at Abbey Road studios in London on July 1, 1963, which was before the group began work on the first tracks for their second album, and by November of that year it had become the first Beatles' single to sell more than a million copies in Britain alone.

The track never appeared on any Beatles' UK studio album but it was included on the American release, *The Beatles Second Album,* after the single, which was released in the States on the independent Swan Records, also became the group's second American number one in March 1964.

The record introduced the world to a very distinctive Beatles' chorus which, according to John, was added because after he and Paul had written the song: "We needed more, so we had 'yeah yeah yeah' and it caught on." When radio presenter Brian Matthew reviewed the single for *Melody Maker* he described it as "banal rubbish", but after it reached number one, he explained that while he at first thought that it might be "a little banal," he conceded it was in fact, a record that "grows on you."

'I WANT TO HOLD YOUR HAND' 'A' LABEL

This limited red label pressing of 'I Want To Hold Your Hand' and the B-side, 'This Boy' was sent out in advance of the official November 29, 1963 release.

Early copies of discs were sent from the EMI factory in Hayes, Middlesex to radio, press and retailers and were marked with a large 'A' in order to identify the A-side for producers, reviewers and stores. They were also stamped 'Demonstration Record Not For Sale' in order that these records, which

as promotional copies were not included in artist royalty calculations, were not subsequently sold on to the public.

The song was recorded at Abbey Road Studios on October 17, 1963 in a total of 17 takes and issued with advance orders of over a million. It replaced 'She Loves You' at number one at the same time as The Beatles also held the number one and two positions on the UK album charts with *Please Please Me* and *With The Beatles*.

AUTOGRAPHS #2

This set of Beatles' autographs includes the signature of Ringo Starr, who joined the band in 1962, and they are dedicated to 'Maureen', which coincidentally was the name of Ringo's first wife – Maureen Cox – who he married in 1965.

Ringo (Richard Starkey) was recruited to join The Beatles as their official drummer in August 1962 after John and Paul turned up at the Butlins Holiday Camp in Skegness – where he was playing with rival Liverpool group Rory Storm & the Hurricanes – and offered him £25 a week to join their band.

He had already deputized on occasions for Pete Best but made his official debut as a Beatle at the Horticultural Society Dance in Port Sunlight, Birkenhead on August 18, 1962. The local advertizing for the concert announced: "playing music with a beat for the Horticultural Society's dance … will be the Beatles, one of the North's leading rhythm groups."

Just over two weeks after that, on September 4, 1962, Ringo joined John, Paul and George at Abbey Road for their first official recording session when they recorded 'How Do You Do It' and 'Love Me Do' under the direction of producer George Martin. It took place in the famous Studio 2 and ran from 7pm through to 10pm in accordance with the studio's strict policy of just three sessions per day, which ran from 10am to 1pm; 2pm to 5pm and then finally 7pm, to 10pm.

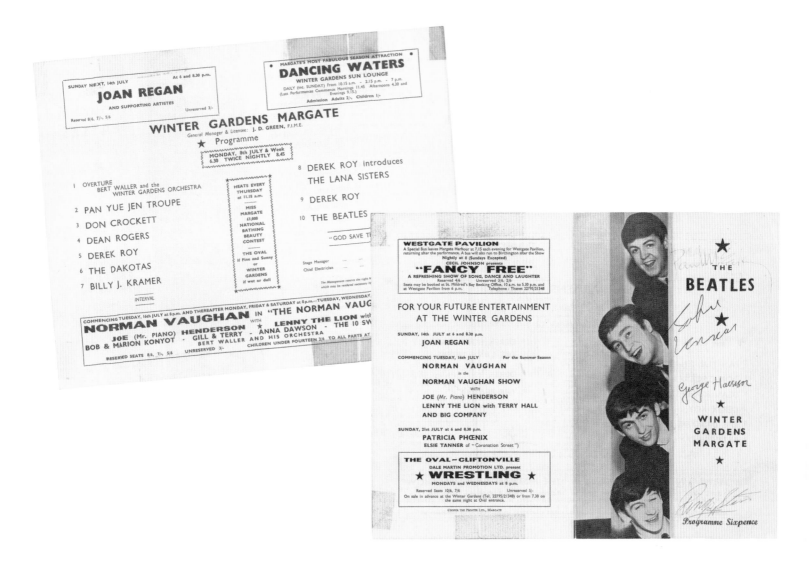

SIGNED PROGRAMME FROM MARGATE

Before they returned to Abbey Road Studios to start work on the tracks for the second *With The Beatles* album, The Beatles travelled to Kent to appear at the famous Winter Gardens in Margate from July 8–13, 1963.

In keeping with their usual demanding schedule, each night they did two shows as part of a ten-week run in British seaside resorts which saw them visit Great Yarmouth, Northwich, Blackpool, Rhyl and Weston Super Mare, Guernsey, Jersey, Llandudno, Torquay, Bournemouth and finally Southport.

This programme comes from Monday July 8, the first night of their week-long stay in Margate, and on the bill alongside The Beatles were Asian dance group the Pan Yue Jen Troupe, who were regulars in British theatre shows and pantomimes in the 1950s

and 1960s, two performers named Don Crockett and Dean Rogers, up-and-coming comedian Derek Roy and Mersey Beat group The Dakotas, who had their own brief spot before teaming up with their more famous front man, Billy J Kramer, ahead of the interval.

The second half featured the trio of The Lana Sisters, who were led by Chantelle Ross (and later famously – and briefly – recruited Dusty Springfield as a member), more comedy from Derek Roy and finally The Beatles, who included Roll Over Beethoven, Thank You Girl, Chains, Please Please Me, A Taste Of Honey, I Saw Her Standing There, Baby It's You, From Me To You and Twist And Shout in their set.

Two days after this show – on July 10 – the Beatles left Margate early in the morning and travelled to London for a

five-hour recording session at the BBC before returning to Kent for their regular two live shows.

The local *Isle of Thanet Gazette* was seemingly less than impressed by the 'fab four' and described their sound as "jungle music" while the official history of the Margate Winter Gardens – which opened in 1911 – proudly states, "the most famous visitors appeared at the Winter Gardens in July 1963; they were the Beatles, destined to become a legend in their own lifetimes."

The Margate programme has a very special meaning for Julian:

"It's from 1963 and that's part of the reason why I decided to get it. The Beatles were all together for six nights in Margate in July, just a few months after I was born (three months earlier on April 8, 1963).

"In those days as up-and-coming musicians you grabbed whatever shows were going – you gotta be seen, you gotta be heard – so you performed in variety and end-of-the-pier shows like this. The same thing happened in the early days of TV – musicians went on entertainment shows in order to be seen."

ROY ORBISON TOUR HANDBILL

From May 18 until June 9, 1963, The Beatles were on tour around Britain with American singing star Roy Orbison and fellow Liverpool group Gerry & the Pacemakers. This advance handbill for the shows in Cardiff put The Beatles as the top act and also had a postal booking form attached.

It was The Beatles' third UK tour that year – already they had been on the road with Helen Shapiro in February and with Tommy Roe and Chris Montez in March – and once again they performed twice-nightly throughout the 21-date tour, which ran from Slough to Blackburn and included a major date at the Liverpool Empire.

Before the tour even started – with Orbison replacing Duane Eddy – there was talk that The Beatles should have been top of the bill but it began with Orbison listed on the cover of the souvenir programme as the top act

above The Beatles – even though they actually closed the show. However, after a week The Beatles had made such an impact that the programme cover was re-printed to put them above Orbison.

Despite selling thousands, if not millions of records by that time, being second on the bill was still a fact of life for The Beatles, according to John: "One of our first big tours was second on the bill to Roy Orbison. It was pretty hard to keep up with that man."

By 1963 Orbison was a major star and had notched up nine UK hit singles, including the number one 'Only The Lonely', written the hit 'Claudette' for the Everly Brothers and established himself as a huge influence on The Beatles, who featured his 1962 hit 'Dream Baby' in their stage act.

Gerry & the Pacemakers – led by Gerry Marsden – were signed to Brian

Epstein's NEMS management company and became the first of the Mersey Beat groups to reach number one in the UK when 'How Do You Do It' (a song The Beatles recorded but refused to release) topped the charts in March 1963 – a month ahead of The Beatles with 'From Me To You'.

Also on the show were British singer David McBeth, who had racked up one top 20 hit in 1959, Louise Cordet, a young girl singer who reached number 13 with 'I'm Just A Baby' in 1962, plus show compère Tony Marsh.

The local newspaper in York carried a review of the May 29 show and confirmed that "Roy Orbison got the biggest hand I've ever heard at the Rialto" but went on to say, "The Beatles were a riot! They could have sung a Liverpool bus time-table and scored a hit." However the *Melody Maker* reviewer saw another show during the tour and reported, "The

quality of Mersey music in the shape of The Beatles and Gerry & the Pacemakers strained me a little on this occasion."

Having seen The Beatles close-up for the first time during the three-week tour, Orbison – who years later would join George Harrison as a member of the Traveling Wilburys – described The Beatles as "just fine" and reckoned success in America was only a matter of time. "If they had a chance to be seen, I think they could be very big. They are the first group from any country playing rock music which never originated in the States," said the star who tragically died in 1988, aged just 52.

1963 PHOTOGRAPHS

Newly-born Julian Lennon is pictured here in the arms of his mum Cynthia and his dad John. The photograph of John with Julian was taken at the home of Aunt Mimi (Smith) in Menlove Avenue, Liverpool. The photograph of Cynthia was taken by her mother, Lilian, in the garden of a bedsit the couple rented.

According to proud mum Cynthia, John's first words when he first held his newborn son were, "Who's going to be a little rocker, just like his dad?" John was not at the birth on April 8, 1963, even though the Beatles did not have a show on that day. They were, however, still busy performing a week after finishing their UK tour with Chris Montez and Tommy Roe, and on April 7 they played the Savoy Ballroom in Southsea and moved on to the Gaumont Ballroom in London's Kilburn district on April 9.

Cynthia Lennon (née Powell) was born in Blackpool in 1939 and first came into contact with John at Liverpool College of Art when she began her studies in 1957. They started dating and she, together with other girlfriends, accompanied John and The Beatles to their shows, including a trip to Hamburg in 1961.

When her own mother emigrated to Canada to act as a nanny to a relation's children, Cynthia moved into a room with John's Aunt Mimi but soon moved out to share a flat with her friend Dot Rhone, who at the time was going out with Paul McCartney. She discovered she was pregnant in 1963 – she and John were married on August 23, 1962 at the Mount Pleasant Registry Office in Liverpool – and Julian was born eight months later. The pair bought the house Kenwood in Weybridge in July 1964 and lived there until they were divorced in November 1968.

'I WANT TO HOLD YOUR HAND' GOLD SINGLE

Set for release in the United States of America in January 1964 as the first Beatles' record to be issued by EMI's US sister company Capitol Records – which had passed on 'Love Me Do', 'Please Please Me', 'From Me To You' and 'She Loves You' – it actually came out on December 27, 1963.

The date was moved after a local disc jockey in Washington DC got hold of a copy of the UK single – which had been issued in November 1963 – from a British airline stewardess and gave it its first US airing ahead of the planned American release schedule. As a result Capitol not only advanced the issue date but also increased the pressing order to 1 million and saw the record become the first US number one by a British act since the Tornados and 'Telstar' in December 1962.

The Beatles heard the news that they had hit the top spot in America for the first time while they were in Paris via a telegram to Brian Epstein from Capitol Records. For John, hitting the US charts with The Beatles was something he had always thought was nigh on impossible. "It just seemed ridiculous – I mean, the idea of having a hit record over there. It was something you could never do."

'CAN'T BUY ME LOVE' GOLD SINGLE

Issued in the UK on March 20, 1964, 'Can't Buy Me Love' became The Beatles' fourth consecutive British number one single.

The record actually came out in America a week earlier and followed 'I Want To Hold Your Hand' and 'She Loves You' to the top spot, giving The Beatles a total of 14 consecutive weeks at number one.

It made the biggest leap in US chart history from number 27 to 1, set a new record of being certified gold on the day of release and, in the week of April 4, 1964, led The Beatles to become the first and only act ever to hold all top five positions in the US chart – ahead of 'Twist & Shout', 'She Loves You', 'I Want To Hold Your Hand' and 'Please Please Me'.

Released with 'You Can't Do That' as the B-side, the single also racked up the highest-ever international advance orders for a record in the history of the music business with 2.1 million sales.

'Can't Buy Me Love' was recorded in Paris at the EMI Pathé Marconi studios on February 29, 1964 during a series of shows in the French capital by The Beatles and during the same one-day session they also completed the German language versions of 'She Loves You' and 'I Want To Hold Your Hand'.

The gold record awards are the original awards presented by the RIAA (Recording Industry of America) to John Lennon as a member of the Beatles at the time the records went gold in the USA (sales of 500,000). These awards are the original white-matte style, so-named because of the white linen background used in the construction of the award. These types of awards were produced from 1963 to 1974 and were strictly limited to the artists only. They are by far the rarest style of all gold record awards and so especially valuable.

Julian has collected a set of the 20 gold discs awarded to the Beatles for sales of their US album releases between 1964 and 1977.

Of the collection, Julian says:

"As far as I know mine is the only full collection of the American gold discs. The idea of the collection is less to do with representing their success and more to do with the gold discs being a complete collection of their work. It was the one thing that I could do that gave me a link with everything they'd done, as bizarrely I don't have a single vinyl album by The Beatles.

"When I first started collecting them the glass in one of them had broken and the gold album had come out of its placement, and I thought I'd try and play it on the record player. That's when I learned that it's not the same album as the one it's supposed to commemorate! All sorts of weird artists and albums have been painted gold and then mounted as somebody else."

'LONG TALL SALLY' DISC

In June 1964 The Beatles released their fifth EP (extended play) record entitled 'Long Tall Sally'. It was originally sold in a mini-album sleeve with a cover photograph by established Beatles' photographer Robert Freeman, who also shot the *With The Beatles* and *A Hard Day's Night* album covers.

This copy has a torn 'Factory Sample Not For Sale' sticker and may have been an advance copy released to radio and press in the cheaper multi-coloured Parlophone singles, bag with the famous £ logo, which was originally a German letter L.

The EP reached number 14 on the British singles chart – the group's four previous EPs had all reached the top 20 – and was significant because it featured only one original Lennon and McCartney song – 'I Call Your Name' – alongside covers of US hit songs 'Long Tall Sally' (by Little Richard), 'Slow Down' (by Larry Williams) and 'Matchbox' (by Carl Perkins).

The title track, written by Enotris Johnson, Otis Blackwell and Richard Penniman (Little Richard) – although only Johnson was credited – and 'I Call Your Name' were recorded on March 1, 1964 and the other two tracks were completed three months later, on June 1, when US rock star Perkins attended the Abbey Road Studios session during his British promo visit, although he did not perform on the record.

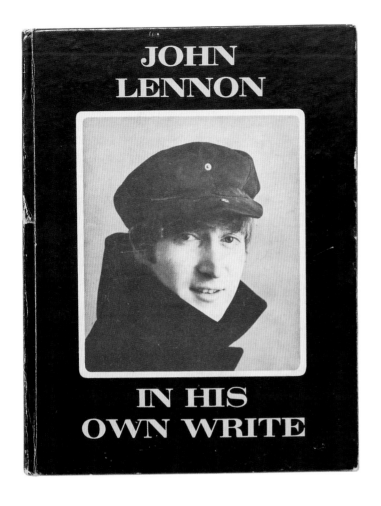

IN HIS OWN WRITE BOOK

Published by Jonathan Cape in UK in March 1964 and described as "a book of nonsense verse and rhyme", this was John Lennon's first book.

It came out as a pocket-sized hardback with a cover photograph by The Beatles' regular photographer, Robert Freeman.

The publication of his first book and its subsequent success – it topped the British best-sellers list with sales of over 100,000 copies – gave Lennon great satisfaction. "I like writing books, I got a kick out of the first one. An awful lot of the material was written while we were on tour, most of it when we were in Margate."

He managed to get the book featured in The Beatles' first film, *A Hard Day's Night*, a move which George described as "the best plug you could have for a book."

On the 4ooth anniversary of William Shakespeare's birth, John was invited to be the guest of honour at the famous Foyles literary luncheon organized by the famous Charing Cross Road booksellers and held at the Dorchester Hotel in London where, in his thank you speech, he said simply, "Thank you very much. You've got a lucky face."

When the book was issued in America in April 1964, John was described by *Time Magazine* as "an unlikely heir to the English tradition of literary nonsense." John had long had a fascination with Lewis Carroll and his writing and drawings also reflected the works of Edward Lear and James Thurber.

The book was described by the renowned *Times Literary Supplement* as, "Worth the attention of anyone who fears for the impoverishment of the English language and the British imagination." Lennon once explained his reason for writing to *Rolling Stone Magazine*, "But to express myself, I would write *Spaniard* or *In His Own Write*, the personal stories which were expressive of my emotions."

Such was the attention focused on Beatle John's literary debut that the work even prompted a debate in the House of Commons in June 1964 when Charles Curran (Conservative, Uxbridge) read to the House from Lennon's poem, 'Deaf Ted, Danoota and me' and suggested it said two things about the author: "He has a feeling for words and storytelling and he is in a state of pathetic near-literacy. He seems to have picked up bits of Tennyson, Browning and Robert Louis Stevenson while listening with one ear to the football results on the wireless."

For Julian the book represented another side to his father's creativity:

"I was just a small boy when it was published and although I probably looked through it, I wouldn't have thought much about it. It was as a teenager that I picked it up again and I started to understand the wit and sarcasm and humour behind it, and that's when I really latched onto it. I didn't get it at first but I could recognize Dad, his zaniness and all that Goons' influence which he loved. I'd seen that side of Dad – the mad side – but it's the combination of creating that into text and drawings. I just thought it was fab. I didn't really equate it to the fact that it was John Lennon, a Beatle and all that – it was just Dad."

A HARD DAY'S NIGHT GRAMMY AWARD

The Beatles' third American number one album turned out to be the first release by the group to win a major US music industry award.

In April 1965 they were awarded the Gramophone Award (or Grammy) by the National Academy of Recording Arts & Science of America (NARAS) for Best Performance By A Vocal Group in 1964 for *A Hard Day's Night* and they also won the award for Best New Artist of 1964. The Beatles went on to win a total of 16 Grammys during the next 44 years, including awards in 2008 for the album *Love* produced for the Cirque du Soleil Las Vegas show of the same name.

Issued in America in June 1964, the album *A Hard Day's Night* reached the top spot after just two weeks on the US album chart and held onto it for a total of 14 weeks but bizarrely the album was never officially certified gold, despite including two million-selling American number one singles – the title track and 'Can't Buy Me Love'.

Also included on the album were four George Martin instrumental versions of Beatles' songs and it remains the only album made up entirely of tracks written by Lennon & McCartney with no cover versions or songs composed by George Harrison.

NATIONAL ACADEMY OF RECORDING ARTS & SCIENCES
THE BEATLES
BEST PERFORMANCE BY A VOCAL GROUP
1964
"A HARD DAY'S NIGHT"

A HARD DAY'S NIGHT
PREMIÈRE TICKETS

The Beatles' first feature film premièred on Monday July 6, 1964 at the London Pavilion theatre in front of HRH Princess Margaret and Lord Snowdon in support of the London Dockland Settlements and the Variety Club Heart Fund.

US film company United Artists were primarily interested in signing The Beatles to their record division when they approached the group with a contract to make three films but were unable to negotiate a deal to switch them from Capitol Records although the soundtrack album from this film did appear in America on the UA label.

The group's debut movie was produced by Walter Shenson, directed by Dick Lester and written by Liverpool writer Alun Owen, while the title line seemingly came from Ringo saying, after a particularly busy day, that he'd had 'a hard's day night' although in

his book, *In His Own Write*, John wrote: "He's had a hard day's night that day, for Michael was a Cocky Watchtower."

The film was shot in and around central London in the Marylebone, Notting Hill and Soho districts, together with scenes filmed in Kew and Gatwick. Among the cast were well-known British actors such as Wilfred Brambell, John Junkin, Norman Rossington, Victor Spinetti and Derek Guyler alongside a young model called Pattie Boyd, who was to become Mrs George Harrison, a couple of years later.

There was also a Northern première of the film at the Odeon cinema in Liverpool on July 10 and the critics, it seemed, were generally favourable about the Beatles' film debut with the writer for American magazine *Village Voice* saying the movie was "the *Citizen Kane* of jukebox movies."

The respected *Halliwell's Film Guide* described *A Hard Day's Night* as: "Comic fantasia with music; an enormous commercial success with the director trying every cinematic gag in the book … At the time it was a sweet breath of fresh air and the Beatles even seemed willing and likeable."

However, American-born director Lester, who made Spike Milligan's debut *The Running, Jumping and Standing Still Film*, and the early pop movie *It's Trad Jazz*, was less than happy with one member of the 'fab four': "John didn't try at all. I noticed this quality he had of standing outside every situation and noting the vulnerability of everyone, including myself. He was always watching."

Speaking to *Rolling Stone*, Lennon gave his own opinion of the movie when he explained, "We were a bit

infuriated by the glibness of it – me witty, Ringo dumb and cute – and were always trying to get it more realistic. But they wouldn't have it."

The Beatles' film deal gave them 25 per cent of the net profits, although a better deal would have been for Epstein to have negotiated for a share of the gross profits. But as The Beatles' manager had originally wanted just a 7.5 per cent share of the net profits, a 25 per cent cut was a good deal as the movie went on to make $14 million on its release and in the UK the soundtrack album held the top spot for a total of 21 weeks.

1964 BEATLES' RECORD PLAYER

When it appeared in America in 1964, this limited edition record player was billed as the "authentic, autographed Beatles phonograph".

It was just one item in the plethora of Beatles' memorabilia that hit the shops in the 1960s although only 5,000 of these record players were ever produced. Costing $29.99 each, the player was only available through US department store Gimbels. The four-speed phonograph featured a colour photograph and the signatures of The Beatles on one half of the lid with a second full-size photograph and more autographs on the inside of

the lid, together with The Beatles' official logo with the extended drop T – as seen on Ringo's drum kit – in the middle.

This deal with Grundig was perhaps one of Epstein's more successful merchandizing ventures involving The Beatles. While he once admitted that "merchandising can be profitable" he also warned, "figures of millions of pounds in royalties from America are undistilled nonsense."

While he did set up deals in the UK for The Beatles to earn from the sales of sweaters, badges, caps, toy guitars, tin trays (5s 9d each and The Beatles

received 2½d – approx 1 pence – per tray), 'Ringo' bread rolls (the royalty was one old penny per roll), Blackpool rock and wallpaper, Epstein also mistakenly entered into a deal in America with a company called Seltaeb (Beatles backwards) giving them the rights to merchandize Beatles' wigs, bubblegum, toy guitars, sweaters, badges and bed sheets. Bizarrely, he negotiated for The Beatles and NEMS to receive only 10 per cent of the income from merchandize sales in America while Seltaeb took 90 per cent.

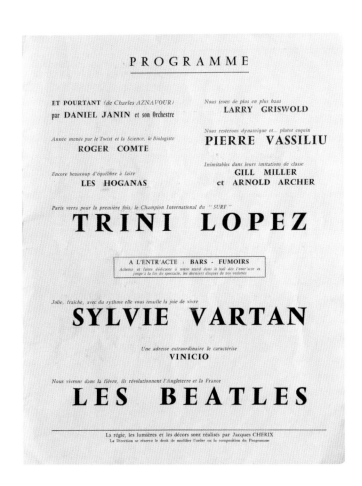

PROGRAMME

ET POURTANT *(de Charles AZNAVOUR)*
par **DANIEL JANIN** et son Orchestre

Année menée par le Twist et la Science, le Biologiste
ROGER COMTE

Encore beaucoup d'équilibre à faire
LES HOGANAS

Paris verra pour la première fois, le Champion International du " SURF "

TRINI LOPEZ

Nous trons de plus en plus haut
LARRY GRISWOLD

Nous resterons dynamique et... plutot coquin
PIERRE VASSILIU

Inimitables dans leurs imitations de classe
GILL MILLER
et **ARNOLD ARCHER**

A L'ENTR'ACTE : BARS - FUMOIRS
Achetez et faites dédicacer à notre stand dans le hall de l'entr'acte et jusqu'à la fin du spectacle, les derniers disques de nos vedettes

---

Jolie, fraîche, avec du rythme elle vous insulte la joie de vivre

SYLVIE VARTAN

Une adresse extraordinaire le caractérise
VINICIO

Nous vivrons dans la fièvre, ils révolutionnent l'Angleterre et la France

LES BEATLES

La régie, les lumières et les décors sont réalisés par Jacques CHERIX
La Direction se réserve le droit de modifier l'ordre ou la composition du Programme

OLYMPIA THEATRE PARIS PROGRAMME

Between January 16 and February 4, 1964, The Beatles took up residence at the world-famous Olympia Theatre in Paris to play two shows daily – and some times even three – for a total of 20 days without a break.

The massive bill featured a total of ten artists, including French singer Sylvie Vartan and American star Trini Lopez, while the group from Liverpool were billed as 'Les Beatles' on the club's now-legendary neon sign.

Reports suggested The Beatles were paid only £50 a show during their three-week stint but while in Paris the group found time to visit the EMI Pathé Marconi studios on January 29 to record German language versions of 'She Loves You' and 'I Want To Hold Your Hand' plus their next international best-seller, 'Can't Buy Me Love'.

Even though they had played a warm-up gig in Versailles on January 15, The Beatles, according to John Lennon, were well aware of the pressures they faced in making their debut at a major French venue. "We have a lot to live up to, especially being top of the bill at the Olympia. If we opened the show and didn't do so well, then we wouldn't have too much to live down."

The show on January 16 was performed to a formal black tie audience of dignitaries and celebrities, including British star Petula Clark, plus French singers Johnny Hallyday, Françoise Hardy and Richard Anthony, and the reception was cool. The *Daily Mail*'s writer suggested, "Beatlemania is still like Britain's entry into the Common Market, a problem the French prefer to put off for a while", while *France Soir* dubbed The Beatles "delinquents" and "has-beens."

Julian Lennon on his collection of Beatles' gold discs:

"The idea of the collectior representing their succes the gold discs being a co their work. It was the one that gave me a link with as bizarrely I don't have The Beatles."

s less to do with

s and more to do with

mplete collection of

thing that I could do

everything they'd done,

a single vinyl album by

MEET THE BEATLES GOLD ALBUM

Meet The Beatles was the second Beatles' album to be released in America and the first by EMI's US company Capitol, who had passed on the group's early UK recordings but were finally persuaded to issue this album on January 20, 1964 with the number Capitol 2047.

In the middle of February 1964 it went to number one in the US and stayed there for 11 weeks, passing the one million sales mark. It contained a collection of nine tracks from the British album release *With The Beatles* plus 'I Saw Her Standing There' (from *Please Please Me*) and the hit single 'I Want To Hold Your Hand' and its B-side 'This Boy'.

The reason for the changes in track listing was that Capitol decided to drop all the cover versions of American songs which appeared on the British album except for 'Till There Was You', which American audiences were familiar with from *The Music Man* and Peggy Lee's hit version of the Meredith Willson song. They did, however, use on the sleeve the same half-light black-and-white portrait shot of The Beatles taken by Robert Freeman for the *With The Beatles* album.

Unimpressed by Capitol's initial reaction to his group, Epstein did the rounds of American record companies in November 1963 and settled on Vee Jay – a label started in 1953 by husband and wife Vivian (Vee) and Jimmy Bracken (Jay), who owned a record store in Chicago – because, he explained, "they had done a good job with Frank Ifield, who was a successful young British star."

The result was that they – and not Capitol – released the first Beatles' album in America, in July 1963, and *Introducing … The Beatles*, which was the US version of the group's debut UK album *Please Please Me*, reached number two in the US charts.

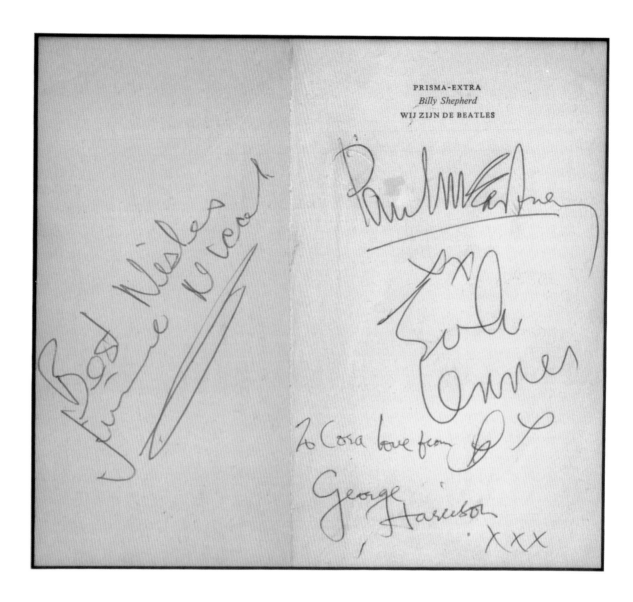

PRISMA-EXTRA
Billy Shepherd
WIJ ZIJN DE BEATLES

AUTOGRAPHS #3

Here, alongside the familiar signatures of John, Paul and George, this set of autographs includes – placed significantly perhaps on a page opposite the other three established Beatles – the message, 'best wishes from Jimmie Nicol'.

On June 3, 1964 Ringo collapsed during a Beatles' photoshoot and was rushed to University College Hospital, where he was diagnosed as suffering from tonsillitis and pharyngitis.

The fact that this was on the very eve of The Beatles' first-ever world tour meant the band was in urgent need of a replacement drummer but producer George Martin could recommend Jimmy (his name was always spelt Jimmy although he signed his autograph as Jimmie) Nicol, who he had recently worked with on a session for Georgie Fame & the Blue Flames. The former Spotniks' drummer

was also known to The Beatles' manager Epstein as he had played on a session with his protégé singer Tommy Quickly.

Nicol was quickly rehearsed and recruited in time for the first two shows on the world tour, in Copenhagen on 4 June. This was followed by a concert on 6 June in the Netherlands, where this set of autographs was collected by a Dutch fan.

Nicol stayed with The Beatles for shows in Hong Kong – where he was mentioned in the *Hong Kong Standard* as being the only Beatle who "braved it outside his hotel room" but was apparently forced back inside by "the rush of teenage fans" – and four concerts in Adelaide, Australia. Ringo rejoined the tour in Melbourne on June 15 and Nicol returned to England but not before a memorable photo session featuring the 'five' Beatles!

THE BEATLES SECOND ALBUM
GOLD ALBUM

The simply and fairly obviously titled *The Beatles Second Album* followed the first from Capitol – *Meet The Beatles* – in April 1964 and went to number one a month later. The album, which was issued with a cover made up of a montage of Beatle shots with the subtitle, "Electrifying big-beat performances", became Capitol's fastest-selling album ever and held on to the top spot for five weeks.

It was once again an American compilation of tracks, including the group's cover versions from *With The Beatles* of classic US rock and pop songs, such as 'Roll Over Beethoven', 'Please Mister Postman', 'You Really Got a Hold On Me', 'Money' and 'Devil In Her Heart' plus the UK EP tracks 'Long Tall Sally' and 'I Call Your Name', alongside the number one hit 'She Loves You' (and its B-side 'I'll Get You') and 'You Can't Do That.'

During its stay at the top *The Beatles Second Album* was joined in the American top three by *Meet The Beatles* and *Introducing ... The Beatles* while two other albums featuring The Beatles also appeared in the lower reaches of the chart – *The Beatles With Tony Sheridan And Their Guests* plus a Vee Jay compilation called *Jolly What! The Beatles & Frank Ifield*.

'A HARD DAY'S NIGHT' GOLD SINGLE

While the album *A Hard Day's Night* swept to number one but failed to register for gold certification in America, the title track single took the top spot and was certified gold when it came out in July 1964, a month ahead of the film's US première at the Beacon Theatre in New York.

It was The Beatles' fifth number one in both the US and the UK between April 1963 and August 1964, although there was a difference in the list of titles – 'I Want To Hold Your Hand', 'She Loves You', 'Can't Buy Me Love' and 'A Hard Day's Night' were all chart toppers in both countries while 'Love Me Do' was an America-only success and 'From Me To You' made up the number in the UK.

'I FEEL FINE' GOLD SINGLE

After dominating the US single charts with five number ones between February and August 1964, the next Beatles' chart topper didn't come along until December when 'I Feel Fine' came out around the same time as the group's fourth UK album, *Beatles For Sale*.

After hitting number one in the UK in early December, the single reached the top spot in America in Christmas week and passed the million sales mark before the start of 1965. It also gave The Beatles an all-time record of 30 US chart entries in a single calendar year.

Airplay for the record in America once again began ahead of the planned schedule when KRLA in Los Angeles got hold of a copy over a month before its official release. Interestingly while 'I Feel Fine' swept to number one, the B-side, 'She's A Woman' rose to number four on the chart thanks to *Billboard*'s policy of including B-sides as chart entries.

SOMETHING NEW GOLD ALBUM

Less than a month after the album from the film *A Hard Day's Night* was released, Capitol issued *Something New*, complete with eight tracks from the original UK soundtrack following an agreement between Capitol and the film company United Artists.

The album spent nine weeks at number two on the US chart and was certified gold even though it never made it to the top spot. The versions of 'Slow Down' and 'Matchbox' from the British 'Long Tall Sally' EP plus the German language version of 'I Want To Hold Your Hand' completed the track listing for a collection that was issued in Europe on the Parlophone label – but was only available through American Armed Forces bases – and in Germany on the Odeon label.

While the cover of the album was created by Capitol for the US market and featured a shot of The Beatles performing on a TV set, it was the constant altering of tracks and the running order of the albums which most annoyed The Beatles and their producer George Martin, who admitted that they had little or no control over how the albums were compiled. "We always objected terribly to what the Americans did to our recordings but I had no say in it," revealed Martin.

JOHN ... AND JULIAN
Two sides of John Lennon: Beatle on
stage (Stockholm, 1964) and father at
home (1966).

TICKET TO RIDE

HIT RECORDS THAT SOLD IN THEIR MILLIONS, CONCERTS PLAYED TO PACKED HOUSES AROUND THE WORLD AND INTERNATIONAL BLOCKBUSTER MOVIES BROUGHT THE BEATLES FAME AND FORTUNE ON A SCALE NEVER BEFORE EXPERIENCED BY ANY BRITISH MUSICIANS. AS THE FAB FOUR CREATED AND PERFORMED THEIR MUSIC SO THE FANS RESPONDED IN THEIR MILLIONS AND WITHIN A FEW MONTHS BEATLEMANIA WAS BORN.

CAPE FROM *HELP!*

The Beatles' second feature film was made in 1965 with the Bahamas and Austria chosen as the locations for filming. As Europe followed the Caribbean in the shooting schedule, John, Paul George and Ringo were under strict instructions not to sunbathe as sporting suntans would have conflicted with the film's storyline.

They were, however, provided with a special wardrobe for the shots on the ski slopes at Obertauern. All four had black skintight trousers and ankle-length ski boots in black sealskin while John sported this black cape lined with white satin.

Cynthia Lennon was in Austria with John when the movie's skiing scenes were shot and recalls The Beatles filming in the Alps. "They had their black hats on, their black capes. They had this amazing setting on this snow-covered mountain with a piano. They didn't exactly ski down the mountains with these torches because they had doubles, but it looked fantastic and every time I see that cape, I remember the whole scenario. We had a lot of fun, a lot of lunacy, a lot of madness and we learned how to ski."

The movie, filmed in colour, was finished on May 13, 1965 and cost $1.5 million to make. The world première was in London on July 29, 1965 with HRH Princess Margaret and Lord Snowdon once again guests of honour. The event raised over £6,000 for charity and there were chaotic scenes in London's Piccadilly Circus where over 10,000 fans were restrained by 200 policemen.

While *Melody Maker* – which gave the acting plaudits to Ringo – suggested that, "… the best scenes were where the Beatles were merely being themselves – on the ski slopes …" and the *Daily Express* observed, "These boys are the closest thing to the Marx Brothers since the Marx Brothers," it seems John was less pleased with the film.

He complained that *Help!*: "was a drag, because we didn't know what was happening … we were on pot then and all the best stuff is on the cutting room floor." He also said, "I was only an extra in my own film."

Halliwell's describes *Help!* as, (an) "exhausting attempt to outdo *A Hard Day's Night* in lunatic frenzy, which goes to prove that some talents work better on low budgets." And they added: "Humour is a frantic cross between *Hellzapoppin*, the Goons, Bugs Bunny and the shades of Monty Python to come."

'HELP!' GOLD SINGLE

When it was released in July 1965, *Help!* was destined to become The Beatles' ninth American number one single (and their eight in the UK) in just under three years. The record held the top spot in America for three weeks from September 4, 1965, nearly a month after the film's US première in New York.

Reflecting on the success of the single and The Beatles in general, John once remarked, "The 'Help!' single sold much better than the two before it 'I Feel Fine' & 'Ticket To Ride'. But there were still a lot of fans who didn't like 'Help!'. We produce something, a record, and if they like it, they get it."

The song was only written after it had been decided that their second film would be entitled *Help!*. Before that it had been called *Beatles Production 2* and then *Eight Arms To Hold You*, but when *Help!* was finally settled on, John and Paul were required to come up with a song that had the same title.

Written almost completely by John, it was recorded in Abbey Road Studios in a single four-hour session during the evening of April 13, 1965 and was described by John as one of his first "message" songs. Speaking to *Rolling Stone Magazine* in 1970, he said, "On *Help!* the lyric is as good now as it was then. It's just me singing 'help' and I meant it."

This letter from John to Cynthia was written during The Beatles' third US tour, which began in New York on August 15 and ended in San Francisco on August 31, 1965.

A personal heartfelt note, it was penned on August 23 during the group's six-day break between concerts which they spent in a rented house in Benedict Canyon, North Hollywood ahead of a show in San Diego on August 28.

It was during this trip that The Beatles had their one and only meeting with Elvis Presley at his Bel Air mansion on August 27. Armed with guitars, bass and piano (but no drums), The Beatles joined Elvis for an improvized rendition of Liverpudlian singer Cilla Black's UK number one single 'You're My World'.

⑥ what we said about it. It's not much bother really, is it? when you think about it — 'cause I'm sure Dot and Lil' and Bernie, Tommy, wee Jackie etc can understand something as simple as us wanting to be alone for a day. — I don't mean Julian tho' — I mean don't pack him off to Dots or anywhere — I really miss him as a person now — do you know what I mean, — he's not so much 'The Baby' or 'my baby' anymore he's a real living part of me now — you know he's Julian and everything and I can't wait to see him, I miss him more than I've ever done before — I think its been a slow process my feeling like a real father! I hope all this is clear and understandable, I spend hours in dressing rooms and things thinking about the times we've wasted not being with him — and playing with him — you know I keep thinking of those stupid bastard times when I keep reading bloody newspapers and other shit whilst he's in the room with me and I've decided it's ALL WRONG! He doesn't see enough of me as it is and I really want him to

① know and love me, and miss me like
I seem to be missing both of you so much.

Still, go now 'cause I'm bringing
myself down thinking what a thoughtless
bastard I seem to be – and it's only sort
of three o'clock in the afternoon and it
seems the wrong time of day to feel so
emotional – I really feel like crying – it's
stupid – and I'm choking up now as I'm
writing – I don't know what the matter with
me – & Its not the tour what's so different
from other tours – I mean I'm having lots
of laughs (you know the type hee! he!) but in
between the laughs there is such a drop – I
mean there seems no in-between feelings.

Anyway I'm going now so
that this letter doesn't get to draggy.
I love you very much.

To Cyn
from
John x x x x x x x
        x x x x x x x
        x x x x x x x

P.S. Say hello to Charles
    etc. for me.

P.P.S. I think you can ring
me if you have a phone there
try – if not I'll see you in about a week.
271-6565
LOS ANGELES,
CALIFORNIA.

P.P.S.
Its Monday the 23rd today
and I leave this house next Monday
the 30th of August – so try to ring

BEATLES '65
GOLD ALBUM

Released in the week before Christmas 1964, the *Beatles '65* album came out just a month after the British *Beatles For Sale* album and sold over three million copies in three weeks as it raced to number one in America less than ten days after its release.

It held the top spot for nine weeks and featured eight tracks from the *Beatles For Sale* album – the missing songs were 'Baby's In Black', 'Kansas City/Hey Hey Hey' medley, 'Words of Love', 'Every Little Thing', 'I Don't Want To Spoil The Party', 'What You're Doing' and 'Eight Days A Week' – plus 'I Feel Fine' and 'She's A Woman', which did not appear on any UK albums.

This was a time when The Beatles and George Martin were becoming more and more annoyed with their American record company continually changing their albums to suit the US

practice of paying royalties on fewer tracks than the number that were traditionally on British albums. This involved taking songs off British albums and collecting them together with records that were released as singles only in the UK to eventually create new albums for the US market.

It was a practice that prompted George to comment, "If you compared the English copy with the American copy you could see that it wasn't as good" while John observed, "They wouldn't let us put 14 (tracks) out, they said there was some rule or something. And so we almost didn't care what happened to the albums in America until we started coming over more …"

'WE CAN WORK IT OUT'
GOLD SINGLE

Released in early December 1965 on both sides of the Atlantic, 'We Can Work It Out' and 'Day Tripper' had the distinction of being the first Beatles' UK single to be officially designated a double A-side and both titles were listed as the number one on the British charts.

In America it was 'We Can Work It Out' which was actually listed at the top of the charts for three weeks in January 1966 while 'Day Tripper' reached number five in the same month.

THE EARLY BEATLES
GOLD ALBUM

When Capitol Records recovered the US distribution rights to The Beatles' earliest recordings from the independent Vee Jay company, they created *The Early Beatles* as a compilation of tracks from 1962 and 1963 which had appeared on the group's British debut album, *Please Please Me*.

Three tracks which had appeared on Vee Jay's 1964 number two album, *Introducing … The Beatles* – 'Misery', 'I Saw Her Standing There' and 'There's A Place' – were left off and replaced by 'Love Me Do' and 'P.S. I Love You'. *The Early Beatles* album, which featured Robert Freeman's cover shot from the *Beatles For Sale* album with a strapline which boasted, "Now On Capitol", was a minor top 50 hit, but was still certified gold.

'EIGHT DAYS A WEEK'
GOLD SINGLE

The song that was at one point considered as the title track for The Beatles' second feature film in the end never even made it onto the soundtrack of the movie, which was eventually called *Help!*.

And while it was never released as a single in the UK, where it appeared on the *Beatles For Sale* album, it came out in America in February 1965 and hit the number one spot a month later after being removed from the *Beatles' 65* album and placed on the subsequent *Beatles VI* release.

The title came not from a quip by Ringo as some have claimed but from Paul's chauffur on a journey to John's house in Weybridge for a writing session. Asked how he was, the driver replied that he was working so hard that he was "working eight days a week."

BEATLES VI GOLD ALBUM

Although it was titled *Beatles VI* – because it was the group's sixth American album from Capitol Records – it was in fact their eighth stateside album release.

Issued in June 1965, it brought together the six tracks from *Beatles For Sale* which did not go on *Beatles '65* plus three songs from the forthcoming *Help!* album and the tracks 'Yes It Is' (B-side of 'Ticket To Ride') and Larry Williams' 'Bad Boy'.

After entering the US top 100 in week one after its release, the album rose to number 48 in week two and then shot to number one on July 10, 1965 where it held onto the top spot for six weeks.

HELP! GOLD ALBUM

Capitol continued their extraordinary policy of changing tracks on The Beatles' American albums when it came to the soundtrack from the group's second film.

In the UK the *Help!* album contained seven songs from the movie on side one and a further seven tracks by The Beatles on side two. In America, where the album was advertised as a "special movie souvenir package", the tracks from side two of the British release were dropped and replaced by instrumental pieces from the film's score, composed and arranged by Ken Thorne and played by the George Martin Orchestra.

Even though his orchestra performed the seven instrumental pieces and he had recorded all the tracks with The Beatles, Martin did not involve himself with the US album version because, as he once explained, " (Dick) Lester engaged Ken

Thorne to do the score and he put the album together in a way I didn't like without my supervision."

Both the US and the UK album featured the same cover photograph by Robert Freeman with The Beatles signalling in semaphore although there were slight differences in the two versions. Freeman's original idea was to have The Beatles spell out the word 'help' but later admitted, "When we came to do the shot, the arrangement of the arms with those letters didn't look good so we decided to improvise and ended up with the best graphic positioning of the arms."

On the UK version The Beatles spelt out the letters NUJV (George = N, John = U, Paul = J, Ringo = V), but for the US version John, Paul and Ringo were moved around to spell out NVUJ.

Julian on the movie Help!:

"It was probably the first fi
absolutely bonkers – thei
clowning about was all
The movie is a piece of h
of him so it holds dear fo
when Dad was at home
place before he disappe
It was a good film too …
surprize to see him skiing

m I saw with them being
madcap humour and
ery much my cup of tea.
tory now and a piece
me. This is from a time
t represents a time and
ared out of my life.
and it was a great
Who'd have thought!"

NASSAU FILM

The Beatles stayed in Nassau in The Bahamas from February 22 until March 9, 1965, during which time they filmed scenes for the movie *Help!*.

This cine film was shot during the group's working visit to the 700 islands that make up The Bahamas and the capital city Nassau. The Beatles stayed in a house in the grounds of the Balmoral Club, close to Cable Beach, and flew out the day after filming finished.

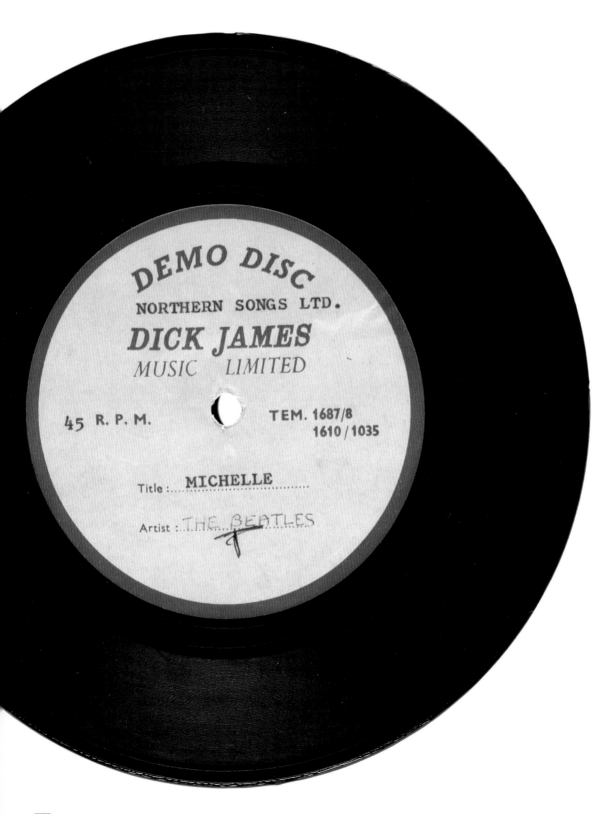

'MICHELLE' ACETATE

An acetate of the song 'Michelle' would have been used by The Beatles and producer George Martin to check the quality of the studio recording of the song when it was transferred to a disc. This copy was produced for The Beatles' music publisher Dick James, who ran their Northern Songs company, and it may have been used to attract other artists or producers to record a cover version.

Acetates were almost always one-sided vinyl discs, kept in plain inner bags and when everybody was satisfied with the quality of the transfer, a 'master disc' would be created and used for the mass production of the record.

'Michelle' was written by Paul and recorded at Abbey Road Studios on November 3, 1965 in just two takes with Paul taking the lead vocal. He later claimed that it was not inspired by any particular person – "I make it up, that's how I write" – and added the famous French lyrics because "I just fancied writing some French words. It was mainly because I always used to think the song always sounded like a French thing."

It featured on both the UK and US versions of the album *Rubber Soul* and has been covered by over 700 artists, including British group the Overlanders, who reached number one in the UK in January 1966.

A SPANIARD IN THE WORKS

John's second book of prose, verse and black-and-white drawings was also published by Jonathan Cape in June 1965. It caused less of a controversy and was considered more adult, less cruel and even cleverer than his first effort.

While explaining that his second book was "more disciplined because it was started from scratch", John was equally delighted to have a second hit on his hands: "*A Spaniard In The Works* gave me another personal boost. OK, it didn't do as well as the first, but then what follow-up book ever does?"

THE PENGUIN JOHN LENNON

John's two published books *In His Own Write* and *A Spaniard In the Works* were brought together by Penguin Books and issued in the UK under the title *The Penguin John Lennon*.

It cost 7s.6d (37p) and featured a cover created by album and song lyric book designer Alan Aldrige, who was one of London's and Apple's favourite graphic designers in the Swinging Sixties.

Julian comments on his signed copy:

"It's amusing to see Dad sign his name O'Lennon because just recently a genealogist told me that the name Lennon derives from the original Irish name O Leannain, which led to O'Lennon and Lennon. Although our family haven't used the O' for 200 years, apparently there's no legal reason why we can't!"

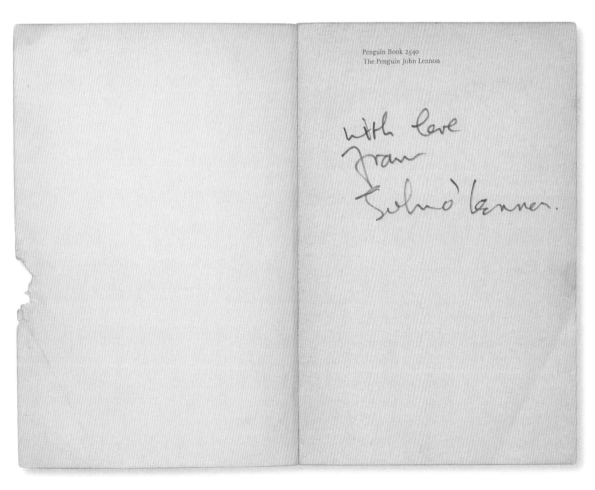

Penguin Book 2540
The Penguin John Lennon

with love
from
John o'lennon.

RUBBER SOUL
GOLD ALBUM

Rubber Soul has a special place in the history of the Beatles' chart topping albums – it was the first of the group's number one releases not to include any single release and it also featured the first use of the Indian string instrument the sitar on a Beatles song, with George playing it on the track 'Norwegian Wood'.

Issued in December 1965 on both sides of the Atlantic, the US version hit the top of the album charts in January 1966 and spent six weeks there while it debuted on the UK chart at number one in it first week of release.

Once again the American album varied from the British title and this time four tracks – 'Drive My Car' / 'Nowhere Man' / 'What Goes On' / 'If I Needed Someone' – were deleted while 'I've Just Seen A Face' and 'It's Only Love' (from UK *Help!* album) were added.

'YESTERDAY'
GOLD SINGLE

The most covered song in the history of popular music was composed by Paul in London and Portugal with the working title 'Scrambled Eggs'. Eventually it became 'Yesterday' but before it was finally recorded – in just two takes at Abbey Road Studios on June 14, 1965 – it had been turned down by two other singers.

Paul first offered the song to British blues singer Chris Farlowe – who decided "I don't like it. It's too soft" – and was then approached by Liverpool singer Billy J Kramer, who was looking for a suitable song for his next recording. He too reckoned the song was "not what he was looking for."

It then became the first Beatles' recording to feature just one of the group as Paul sang and played guitar accompanied by a string quartet, although it seems that George was in the studio during the session but did not appear on the record.

'Yesterday' was only issued as a single in America, where it went to number one for four weeks in October 1965 and featured Ringo's version of Buck Owens' hit 'Act Naturally' as the B-side. While the song appeared on the UK version of *Help!*, it did not appear on an American album until July 1966.

There have been over 2,500 cover versions of 'Yesterday', which was honoured as the most played British song in America when it racked up over seven million airings on US TV and radio, with Matt Monro reaching number eight in the UK in 1965.

OPPOSITE //

REVOLVER NOMINATION
CERTIFICATE

NARAS (National Academy of Recording Arts & Sciences of America) issued The Beatles with this certificate to acknowledge the nomination of their album *Revolver* for the award as Album of the Year in 1966.

While Revolver didn't win a Grammy for Best Album, it did collect the prize for Best Album Cover, recognizing the work of German designer and musician Klaus Voorman, who had first seen The Beatles in Hamburg in 1960 when he hung around backstage to show the group his designs for a record cover.

After learning to play bass guitar, he moved to England and joined the trio Paddy Klaus & Gibson, who eventually became part of Brian Epstein's management stable. After they split up he moved on to work with the group Manfred Mann before returning to design work – the *Revolver* cover was created alongside album sleeves for George Harrison, Jackie Lomax and the Bee Gees. In 1995 he was invited to design the covers for The Beatles three *Anthology* albums.

REVOLVER
GOLD ALBUM

The last album that The Beatles recorded while still a touring band, *Revolver* came out in America on August 8, 1966, just three days after its release in the UK.

For once there were no extra tracks added to the American version although three songs – 'I'm Only Sleeping,' 'And Your Bird Can Sing' and 'Doctor Robert' – were removed to bring the US track listing down to 11. It reached number one in America after just two weeks on the chart and held the top spot for six weeks, earning The Beatles 17 weeks at number one in 1966 with three albums.

THE NATIONAL ACADEMY
OF
RECORDING ARTS AND SCIENCES

presents this certificate to

THE BEATLES

in recognition of

NOMINATION

for the

ALBUM OF THE YEAR

REVOLVER

for the awards period

1966

George Avakian
PRESIDENT

YESTERDAY AND TODAY
GOLD ALBUM

According to George Harrison, the albums *Revolver* and *Rubber Soul* were, "A continuation of each other. They could actually be blended into one album because they have a similar sound."

Whether or not they took his views on board, Capitol decided to take three tracks from the first album and four from the second and build them into the US-only collection *Yesterday And Today*, which also featured the US number one hit 'Yesterday' – and its B-side, 'Act Naturally' (from *Help!*) – plus the track 'We Can Work It Out'.

Issued on June 29, 1966, it reached the number one spot in four weeks and held onto it for a further five, although there was a change of cover along the way. The album had originally been released with what became known as the 'butcher's cover' shot, which featured The Beatles in bloody lab

coats with pieces of raw meat and cut-up plastic dolls.

Protests from the public and the American record trade forced Capitol to withdraw the sleeve and replace it with a safer photograph of the group sitting around a shipping suitcase with Paul crouched inside. Executives at Capitol explained the original cover had been created in England and was intended as pop art satire but was "subject to misinterpretation."

The original, but eventually withdrawn album cover shot was taken in London in March 1966 at the Chelsea studio of photographer Robert Whittaker, who had photographed fellow Liverpudlian acts Billy J Kramer, Cilla Black and Gerry & the Pacemakers and was also involved with the creation of the *Revolver* sleeve and Cream's *Disraeli Gears* album cover.

It appeared in colour as the cover of

Disc music paper on June 11, 1966 and was an image that John in particular wanted to see used as an album cover: "I wanted to show that we were aware of life and I was really pushing for that album cover. I would say that I was a lot of the force behind it going out and trying to keep it out."

The situation wasn't helped by the fact that the album came out in the midst of The Beatles also suffering a major backlash in America over remarks made by John in March 1966, when he suggested the group were "more popular than Jesus." As a result of his comments, Beatles' records were banned from US radio stations and pubic bonfires were organized, where records, photos and memorabilia were burned, while in South Carolina the Klu Klux Klan attached a Beatles' record to a burning cross.

'NOWHERE MAN'
GOLD SINGLE

Recorded on October 21 and 22, 1965, 'Nowhere Man' featured on the UK album *Rubber Soul* and on *Yesterday And Today* in the US, where it was also released as a single in February 1966.

It plugged the six-month gap between number one hits 'We Can Work It Out' and 'Paperback Writer', but only managed to reach number three in the charts in March 1966 while a cover version by the trio, 'Three Good Reasons', hit the UK top 50 in the same month.

John once recalled that he came up with the idea while sitting around at home trying to find inspiration for a song that, in his words, was "meaningful and good." When he realized that he was doing nothing and going nowhere, he thought of himself as "Nowhere Man."

'YELLOW SUBMARINE'
GOLD SINGLE

'Yellow Submarine' was recorded over two days – May 26 and June 1, 1966 – in Abbey Road Studios with the second day set aside for the extraordinary collection of sound effects that were laid behind Ringo's lead vocal.

Recruiting studio staff and more famous visitors such as Rolling Stone Brian Jones, Marianne Faithfull and Patti Harrison as helpers, together with assistants Neil Aspinall and Mal Evans, the extra sounds included bells, whistles, clinking glasses and chains rattled in a bath of water.

The track was issued as a double A-side with 'Eleanor Rigby', which was recorded in 15 takes on April 28, 1966 and became The Beatles' second double A-sided UK number one in August and gave Ringo his first chart topper as a vocalist.

In America it peaked at number two in September 1966.

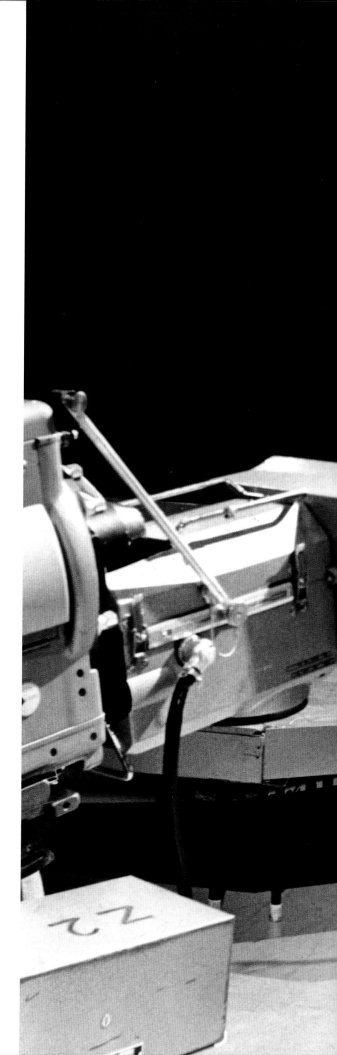

'PAPERBACK WRITER' GOLD SINGLE

Completed in just days at Abbey Road Studios in April 1966, 'Paperback Writer' leapt to the top of the American charts in just three weeks in June 1966 to become the group's twelfth US chart topper and their tenth in the UK.

It was once described by John as "Son of 'Day Tripper' – meaning a rock 'n' roll song with a guitar lick on a fuzzy, loud guitar."

SKETCH BY JOHN LENNON

John had a long history of producing drawings which went back to his school days and developed during his time at the Liverpool College of Art, which he attended from September 1957 until May 1960, when he left following the Silver Beatles' tour of Scotland with singer Johnny Gentle.

While a pupil at Quarry Bank High School, John involved himself in the creation of a book called *Daily Howl*, which featured his writing and drawings, including what would later be described as "octopoid grotesques" when they came up for consideration for inclusion in his first book, *In His Own Write*.

He also wrote for the Liverpool music paper *Mersey Beat*, which had been launched by fellow Art College student Bill Harry in 1961, where the column 'Beatcomber' – a tribute to the famous *Daily Express* column – was created as a

vehicle for his articles and drawings.

Years later John admitted to being inspired by English illustrator Ronald Searle and recalled working with a black pen or an ordinary fountain pen with black ink: "So when it came to doing the book I said, 'Well, I can draw, as well you know'; the drawings were very scrappy because I'm heavy handed. I just start to draw and if it looks like something vaguely to do with the story, I do it."

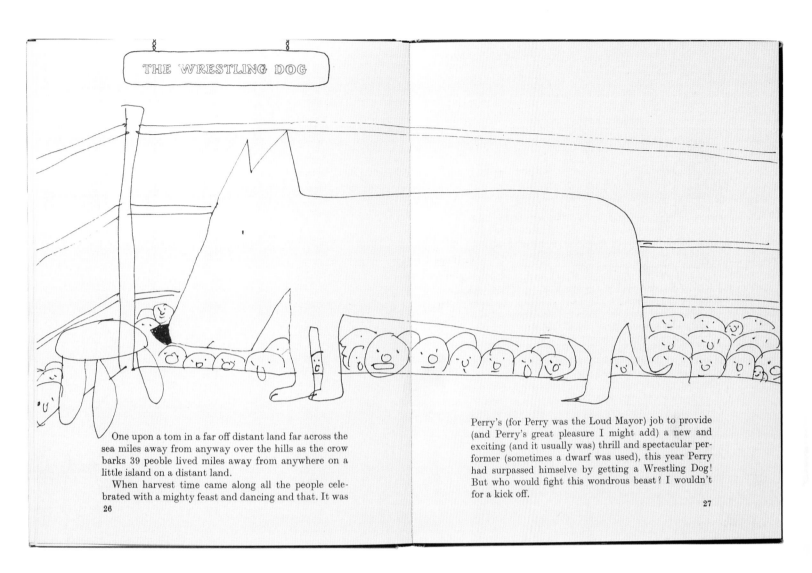

THE WRESTLING DOG

One upon a tom in a far off distant land far across the sea miles away from anyway over the hills as the crow barks 39 peoble lived miles away from anywhere on a little island on a distant land.

When harvest time came along all the people celebrated with a mighty feast and dancing and that. It was

26

Perry's (for Perry was the Loud Mayor) job to provide (and Perry's great pleasure I might add) a new and exciting (and it usually was) thrill and spectacular performer (sometimes a dwarf was used), this year Perry had surpassed himselve by getting a Wrestling Dog! But who would fight this wondrous beast? I wouldn't for a kick off.

27

Julian on his father's drawings:

"They were strange creatures and it was very definitely a specific style he had with his characters. I was always quite curious about that because I wondered where those kinds of images came from. I mean, how did he come up with those images?

"I know people talk about them being cruel but I have never looked at them as being particularly cruel. I always took it and looked at it purely from a humorous side, a joke, a big laugh. I never saw it as being cruel although he probably meant what he said and drew. Looking at the book, I think that maybe it shows that he didn't really care what people thought.

"The drawings allowed you to perhaps get more of an insight into his words and what he was thinking of - you were getting a visual, not just the text, just in case you didn't quite get it, just to help you along maybe ..."

BEATLES SHEA STADIUM TICKETS

This pair of (unused) tickets are from The Beatles' second and final appearance at Shea Stadium on August 23, 1966 when 11,000 seats in the 56,000-seater arena remained unsold.

Even though the famous stadium in New York's Queens district was not full, The Beatles took a massive 65 per cent of the gross receipts ($292,000) and earned a new high of $189,000 from their night's work at the home of the New York Mets baseball team.

The Beatles arrived in New York on the back of 14 concerts in Chicago, Detroit, Cleveland, Washington DC, Philadelphia, Toronto, Boston, Memphis, Cincinnati and St Louis. They were driven to the stadium in a Wells Fargo security truck and left for Los Angeles immediately after the concert. After a further three concerts in Seattle and Los Angeles, the Beatles played their last-ever live concert on August 29, 1966 in San Francisco's Candlestick Park.

A year earlier The Beatles opened their third American tour at Shea Stadium on August 15 and then the concert took place in front of 55,000 people with record takings of $306,000 – "the greatest gross ever in the history of show business" according to show promoter Sid Bernstein – and The Beatles' share was a then world record $160,000.

In 1965 The Beatles travelled the five miles from Manhattan to the nearby World's Fair site by helicopter and were then transported to the venue by armoured truck for their 30-minute performance, which featured 13 songs.

According to John, Shea Stadium in 1965 was an extraordinary experience: "It was the biggest crowd we ever played to, anywhere in the world. And it was fantastic, the most exciting we've ever done. Once you plug in and the noise starts, you're just a group playing anywhere again and you forget that you're The Beatles."

A year on, and with thousands of tickets for their second appearance at Shea Stadium unsold, The Beatles, according to producer George Martin – made a major decision about their future as a touring group. "Curiously enough the second Shea Stadium concert had about 11,000 seats unsold. So it was a pretty unsettling time. And it was against this background that they said, 'Right, we definitely won't do any more'."

JULIAN, PAUL AND JOHN
Opposite: These photographs, taken by
Terry Doran, a friend of John and
Cynthia, show four-year-old Julian with
Paul on the set of *Magical Mystery Tour*.
Paul is wearing his wizard costume from
the film. Above: Julian and John
together at home at Kenwood.

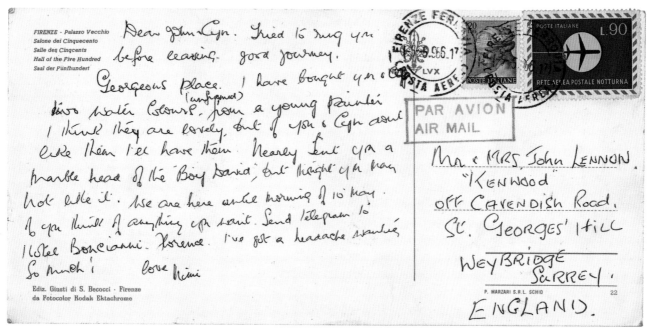

POSTCARD FROM MIMI, 1966

A postcard sent by Aunt Mimi from her holiday in Florence in 1966 to John and Cynthia at their Kenwood home in Weybridge, Surrey.

Mimi (Mary Smith) was John's Aunt and one of his mother Julia's four sisters, who married dairy farmer George Smith. She brought John up from the age of five, when he left his mother's home and moved into her semi-detached house in Menlove Avenue, Liverpool.

After the death of her husband, who died when John was 12, Mimi looked after him on her own and even bought

him his first guitar, although she did famously warn him that the instrument was alright as a hobby, "but you'll never make a living out of it."

When he and the other Beatles 'made it', John showed his appreciation by buying Mimi a bungalow in Poole, where she lived until her death at the age of 88 on December 6, 1991 – two days before the eleventh anniversary of John's death in New York in 1980.

MAGICAL MYSTERY TOUR

WHEN THEY RETIRED FROM PLAYING LIVE, THE BEATLES TRAVELLED ALONG A NEW ROUTE WHICH SAW THEM FOCUS THEIR ATTENTION ON PROJECTS AND IDEAS – SOME CRAZY AND SOME SENSIBLE – WHICH STRETCHED THEM BOTH CREATIVELY AND PERSONALLY. WHETHER THEY WERE IN THE RECORDING STUDIO, BEHIND AND IN FRONT OF THE CAMERAS OR SIMPLY CONTEMPLATING THE LIVES THEY WERE LIVING, THE BEATLES WERE INTENT ON MOVING ON.

AFGHAN COAT FROM MAGICAL MYSTERY TOUR AND PINSTRIPE TROUSERS

John famously wore this coat at the height of the Swinging Sixties both at the launch party for The Beatles' *Sgt. Pepper's Lonely Hearts Club Band* album and on the set of their film *Magical Mystery Tour*, where he also wore the pinstripe trousers as part of a suit and together with the Afghan coat – plus a pair of fashionable brown and white brogues.

Cynthia Lennon recalls seeing John in the coat during the early days of British psychedelia: "I can picture him now with his round granny glasses and the slight beard or moustache, wearing home that coat and all the jewellery."

At some point John gave the coat to his friend Harry Nilsson but as it didn't fit him, he passed it on to his sister Michelle, who was later told by John, "take good care as it will be valuable one day."

Magical Mystery Tour was first announced in September 1967 and described as "a four-day coach trip of the South of England picking random locations and filming an hour-long TV show", and it seemed that at the time The Beatles were confident it would be screened in Britain over the Christmas period.

It was eventually broadcast by the BBC in black and white on December 26, 1967 at 8.35pm with the added news that a "colour version will be seen on BBC2 within a fortnight of the Boxing Day screening."

In its programme listings section for Christmas 1979, the BBC's very own *Radio Times* announced: "The Beatles Present Their Own Film * *Magical Mystery Tour* with songs and music from John Lennon, Paul McCartney, George Harrison, Ringo Starr * starring The Beatles with Ivor Cutler, Jessie Robins, Mandy Weet, Nat Jackely, Victor Spinetti * devised, written and directed by The Beatles."

In the same issue was a separate feature story which proclaimed: "Yes this is it. Probably the most talked-about TV film of the year. It is by the Beatles and about the Beatles. The story? A coach trip around the West Country reflecting the Beatles' moods, and also launching a handful of new songs. This is the first time the Beatles have produced and directed their own film. How has it turned out? Tonight you can find out by joining the MMTour."

In fact, around 13 million British viewers tuned in to see what the MMTour was about, but the critical reviews put off US broadcasters who turned down the opportunity to air the film. *Time Magazine* wrote, "Paul directed, Ringo mugged, John did imitations, George danced a bit and, when the show hit the BBC last week, the audience gagged."

At the same time the TV critic of the popular *Daily Express* newspaper declared he had never seen "such blatant rubbish" while the headline in the tabloid *Daily Mirror* read, "No magic in this sad Beatles' tour" and the *Daily Mail* proclaimed, "It's colossal, the conceit of the Beatles."

Ringo told *Melody Maker* in 1971 that he thought *Magical Mystery Tour* was Paul's idea. "It was one sheet of paper with a circle on it and it was marked like a clock, only there was only one o'clock, five o'clock, nine o'clock and 11 o'clock, the rest we had to fill in. That's how we did that."

Paul had earlier explained, "We thought the title was explanation enough. There was no plot and it was formless – deliberately so and those people expecting a plot were probably disappointed."

The tour of the West County in a coach was reminiscent of a traditional day trip in a charabanc but this one came with a collection of larger-than-life characters, including a fat lady, four dwarfs, an accordionist, a starlet, the tour courier, a coach trip fan and an amateur photographer. The actors who played these parts and left London on the bus on September 11, 1967 were joined along the way by Paul's brother Mike McGear, the Apple electronics wizard Alexis Mardas and pop star Spencer Davis and his family.

The Afghan jacket is part of a distant memory for Julian from The Beatles' Magical Mystery Tour:

"I know I was on set and there are lots of pictures of me, for example with Paul, and you can see me on the coach in the actual film, but I don't remember much, really. I was only four and it's all a bit of a blur to me and what I do remember is more impressionistic – that it was all just a bit crazy.

"I haven't watched *Magical Mystery Tour* for ten years or more and I'd be curious to go back and watch it now, though I don't know how much sense I'd make of it. I don't think The Beatles had much of a clue themselves as to what it was all about, but it looks like they had an incredible time making it!"

In all, 43 people toured Devon and Cornwall on the coach while extra filming was done in an RAF station in Kent, Paul Raymond's Revue Bar strip club in London and a hilltop in France. The six original songs that The Beatles performed in the film were all shot on location.

The film cost The Beatles a total of £75,000 to make and was described by John as "the most expensive home movie ever" although he added, "I don't regret *Magical Mystery Tour*. I think it was great, I think it'll prove that in the end. But I enjoyed the fish-and-chip quality of *Mystery*. The fact that we went out with a load of freaks and tried to make a film is great, you know."

Before the film was shown on television at Christmas 1967, The Beatles issued the songs from *Magical Mystery Tour* ('Magical Mystery Tour', 'The Fool On The Hill', 'Flying', 'Blue Jay Way', 'Your Mother Should Know' and 'I Am The Walrus') as a double EP and it reached number two in the UK singles chart four days after the movie was broadcast.

In their advertisement for the new release, EMI Records offered the record-buying public a chance to acquire: "A 32-page full-colour book packed with exclusive pictures – a strip cartoon of the *Magical Mystery Tour* story – plus the words to the songs in the show. Buy the *Magical Mystery Tour* book and record complete for only 19s 6d."

As EPs were not popular in America, Capitol chose to create a *Magical Mystery Tour* album, which meant adding as extra tracks 'Hello Goodbye', 'Strawberry Fields', 'Penny Lane', 'Baby You're a Rich Man' and 'All You Need Is Love'. The album topped the US charts in January 1968 and stayed there for eight weeks while it also reached the UK top 30 as an import in the same month, despite the BBC banning the track 'I Am The Walrus' over the use of the word 'knickers'.

Speaking in the month *Magical Mystery Tour* came out, John told *Rolling Stone*, "Records can't be seen so it's good to have a film of some sort to go with the new music."

'ALL YOU NEED IS LOVE'
GOLD SINGLE

In 1967 The Beatles were chosen to represent the BBC – and presumably Britain – in the worlds' first television satellite linkup with a global audience of over 400 million.

The song they wrote for the event was 'All You Need Is Love', which was released in America on July 17, 1963 and went straight to number one in August. In the UK, the single was issued ten days earlier.

The first recording session for the *Our World* television programme took place in Olympic Sound Studios, London, on June 14, when an initial backing track was taped and work continued in Abbey Road on June 24, the eve of the broadcast.

The next day The Beatles, producer George Martin plus guests Mick Jagger, Keith Richards, Brian Jones, Graham Nash, Keith Moon and Donovan – and a 13-piece orchestra conducted by Mike

Vickers – assembled in Abbey Road's number one studio to perform and tape the six-minute live performance of 'All You Need Is Love'.

The version of the song released as a single was actually re-recorded in the evening after the television show had been completed, when John added a new vocal and the song was edited down to four minutes.

According to producer George Martin, Brian Epstein appeared one day with the news that The Beatles were to represent Britain in a round-the-world television hook-up and they needed to write a new song. "We had less than two weeks to get it together and then we learnt that there were going to be over 300 million people watching," recalls the man who organized the famous session in Abbey Road. "John came up with the idea of the song which was ideal, lovely."

SGT. PEPPER'S LONELY HEARTS CLUB BAND GOLD ALBUM

From August 1966, the Beatles focused their attention on studio recording and between December 1966 and April 1967, they worked on a new album that was destined to change both the look and sound of popular music.

Sgt. Pepper's Lonely Hearts Club Band took close to 700 hours to record, cost around £25,000 and, following its release in the first week of June 1967, it was the first Beatles' album to be released simultaneously worldwide and the first to appear in America without any changes to the track listing. It went to number one in America for 15 weeks, while in Britain it hit the top spot on no fewer than four separate occasions

over eight months between June 1967 and February 1968.

In the first week of its release in the UK, the album sold over 250,000 copies and passed the half million mark within a month, while in America it sold over 2.5 million copies in three months.

However, *New Musical Express* editor Andy Gray aired some reservations in his June 1967 review: "Whether the album is their best yet I wouldn't like to say after one hearing. Whether it was worth the five months it took to make I would also argue. But it is a very good LP."

While no singles were issued from the album, controversy still surrounded The Beatles' tenth US number one and their eighth British chart topper when the BBC

banned the track, 'A Day In The Life' because they thought it might encourage drug taking while 'Lucy In The Sky With Diamonds' was linked with the drug LSD. Paul's response to the BBC ban was to explain to the press, "We don't care if they ban our song. It might help the LP."

Although *Sgt. Pepper* was labelled the world's first concept album, John was less than convinced about the description: "… it doesn't go anywhere. All my contributions to the album have absolutely nothing to do with this idea of *Sgt. Pepper* and his band, but it works because we said it worked and that's how the album appeared."

Although only four when it was released, the album made an impact on Julian:

"It is the ultimate Beatles' album for me. It crossed so many boundaries and brought a lot of different influences and styles together all in one album, which was the first time I'd heard something like that, and the production on it was unlike any stuff I'd heard before. Without a doubt it is still a big favourite.

"I've always tried to write songs where the meaning and emotion of the music and lyrics marry into one song that anyone can relate to. One of the things that The Beatles did in particular was exactly that."

SIGNED *SGT. PEPPER* COVER

Sgt. Pepper's Lonely Hearts Club Band was not only a landmark album, it also broke most of the rules regarding album cover design. It was one of the earliest gatefold sleeves, included a pull-out-and-keep set of cut outs – of a moustache, a picture card, a set of sergeant's stripes, two badges and a Beatles' stand-up – and was the first album sleeve with printed song lyrics.

This is a rare signed copy – autographed by all four Beatles – of the cover, which was designed by artist Peter Blake, who was knighted in 2002, and photographed by Michael Cooper.

The original idea for the sleeve of *Sgt. Pepper* followed each of The Beatles being asked to list their 12 favourite

heroes from history but the final work does not include all the people chosen by the group while it does feature various unknown characters and some people chosen by the designers.

The montage was assembled by Blake and photographed in Cooper's studio in Flood Street, Chelsea, where he also created the cover for The Rolling Stones album, *Their Satanic Majesties Request.*

While the likes of Marlon Brando, Lenny Bruce, W.C. Fields, Fred Astaire, Edgar Allen Poe, Bob Dylan, Sir Robert Peel, Tony Curtis, Marilyn Monroe, Karl Marx, H.G. Wells, Dylan Thomas, Max Miler, Bob Dylan, Laurel & Hardy, Albert Einstein, Tom Mix, Oscar Wilde, Lewis Carroll and Sonny Liston all appear,

John's initial choices of Adolf Hitler and Jesus Christ – according to Paul this was John being "bold and brassy" and "into risk taking" – were turned down while EMI asked that Gandhi be removed in order not to offend people in India.

So wide ranging was the list of celebrities to be included on the cover that EMI insisted The Beatles wrote to all the people they wanted to feature on the sleeve to get their permission. This task fell to those in manager Epstein's office and it seems that they spent hours sending notes to all the people pictured, asking them to sign if they agreed to be included.

Veteran American actress Mae West was one of those who refused, but when

all four Beatles signed a personal note asking her to reconsider, she then agreed.

For Julian the album artwork set new boundaries in sleeve design:

"The cover was pretty phenomenal, too: out there and completely different from anybody else's. It definitely pushed the boundaries. I'd heard the story that one of The Beatles called up Mae West to get permission to use her image on the cover, but I'm not sure which one it was – if it had been Dad, he would definitely have been cheeky and Paul would have been the smooth talker."

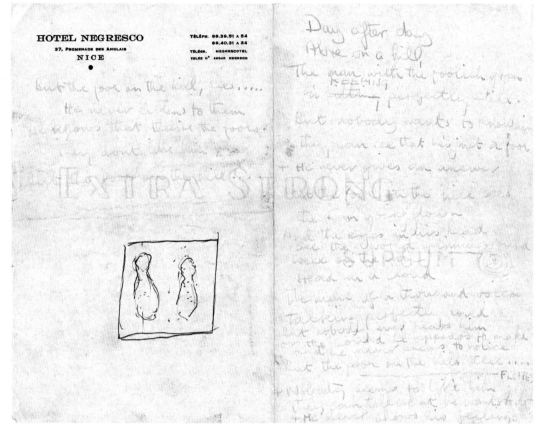

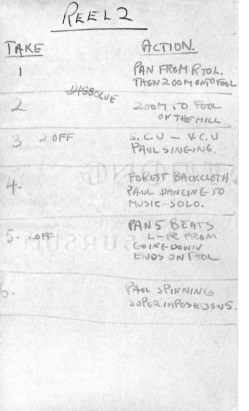

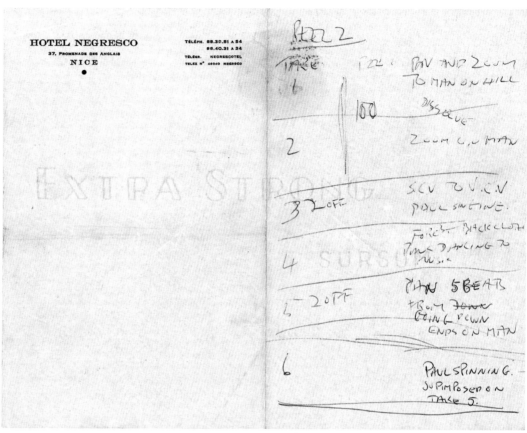

'THE FOOL ON THE HILL' LYRICS

Paul wrote 'The Fool On The Hill' for the *Magical Mystery Tour* film and recorded it at Abbey Road Studios on five separate days in September and October 1967, when The Beatles were joined by three flautists on the final session.

The sequence for the film was shot in Provençe in the South of France on October 30 and 31, 1967, ten days after the last session in Abbey Road and it seems that Paul wrote out these story-board notes on headed stationery from a nearby Nice hotel.

Apparently inspired by a cave-dwelling hermit or guru, he once said he thought he was writing about "someone like Maharishi", who was sometimes called a fool by his critics, while John once observed, "Now that's Paul. Another good lyric. Shows he's capable of writing compete songs."

A year after The Beatles' recording, Brazilian act Sergio Mendes and Brazil 66 hit the US top ten with their version of the song; while in Britain, Shirley Bassey reached the top 50 in 1971.

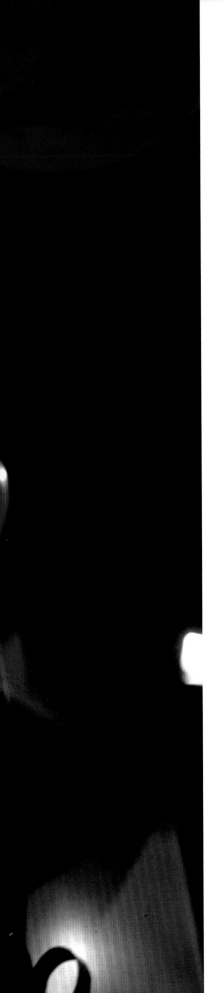

'HELLO GOODBYE' GOLD SINGLE

Although The Beatles began recording 'Hello Goodbye' during the making of *Magical Mystery Tour*, it was never intended for use in the film although a song from the movie – 'I Am The Walrus' – was featured as the B-side.

Released in both the US and the UK in the last week of November 1967, 'Hello Goodbye' reached number one in America in the last week of December and stayed there for three weeks while in Britain it equalled The Beatles' record of seven weeks at number one – tying with the 1963 hit, 'From Me To You.'

While there is a suggestion that John was less than pleased that his surreal Lewis Carroll-inspired classic 'I Am The Walrus' was issued as the flip of Paul's more catchy effort, 'Hello Goodbye', it was the BBC's decision to ban another of his songs – this time because of the word "knickers" – that genuinely irked him: "Every bloody record I put out was banned by the BBC for some reason or another. Even 'Walrus' was banned on the BBC at one time because it said 'knickers'. We chose the word because it is a lovely expressive word. It rolls off the tongue."

'PENNY LANE'/'STRAWBERRY FIELDS' GOLD SINGLE

Before they embarked on *Sgt. Pepper*, The Beatles apparently toyed with the idea of making a concept album about Liverpool and selected 'Penny Lane' and 'Strawberry Fields' as two 'musical' land-marks in the city.

Penny Lane was a local bus round-about with a barber's shop (called Bioletti's) near Paul's home, while Strawberry Fields was the site for a children's community home run by the Salvation Army and close to John's childhood home.

When they began work on *Sgt. Pepper*, both tracks were considered for inclusion on the album but eventually they were released as a double A-side single. Paul's 'Penny Lane' was recorded in Abbey Road over seven days between December 29, 1966 and January 17, 1967, while John's 'Strawberry Fields' was started on November 24 and finished on December 22, 1966 after nine sessions.

Considered by many to be the finest single record ever made, it was released in both the US and the UK in the middle of February 17, 1967 and 'Penny Lane' reached number one in America in March after advance orders of over a million.

'LUCY IN THE SKY WITH DIAMONDS'

Julian Lennon was just four years of age when he completed the drawing which inspired The Beatles to produce a track on the *Sgt. Pepper* album called 'Lucy in the Sky With Diamonds'.

It had been painted at his local nursery school and featured his class friend Lucy O'Donnell. John was always adamant that it contained no drug references: "My son Julian came in one day with a picture he painted about a school friend of his named Lucy. He had sketched in some stars in the sky and called it 'Lucy in the Sky With Diamonds'. Simple."

Beatles' producer George Martin was equally convinced of the song's origins when he said, "It had absolutely nothing to do with LSD and everything to do with the mind of a child", while Paul remembers seeing the painting soon after Julian brought it home.

"I went up to John's house in Weybridge. When I arrived we were having a cup of tea and he (John) said: 'Look at this great drawing Julian's done. Look at the title.' He showed me a drawing on a piece of school paper of a little girl with lots of stars and right across the top there was written in very neat child handwriting, Lucy in the Sky With Diamonds.

"And we loved it and she was in the sky and it was very trippy to us. So we went upstairs and started writing it. People later thought 'Lucy in the Sky with Diamonds' was LSD, I swear we didn't notice that when it came out."

The song's surreal lyrics reflected the love both John and Paul had for Lewis Carroll's *Alice In Wonderland* book and Paul once confirmed, "And in our mind it was an Alice thing, which both of us loved."

Despite the group's protestations and denials about links with LSD and confirmation of the influence of Carroll in their work, the BBC still took it upon themselves to ban 'Lucy In the Sky With Diamonds' because of the supposed drug connections.

For Julian the drawing still brings back memories of his childhood:

"**Looking at the drawing again definitely brings back a time and a place. I kinda have a photographic memory with certain elements in life – sort of like a video playback – I can see myself almost from a third person point of view. Every time I see the Lucy drawing it brings back memories of the time period I did it, although I don't remember the exact time when I did it. Lucy and I clicked even as kids and we were always the two little kids in the corner painting or laughing or just having a good time.**

"**I have no idea how the phrase 'Lucy in the Sky With Diamonds' came about – shiny things in the sky probably become diamonds when you are just four or five years old.**

"**At school I always had an interest in art and that's mainly from both Mum and Dad being at art school. I just felt that there should be some of that in me, I think. I did used to sketch at school with doodles and the like, but I never pursued Dad's style, although Sean has taken a liking to that sort of sketch art, obscure and sometimes bizarre images, not dissimilar to Dad's actually.**

"**The original Lucy drawing is owned by someone else, but as I drew it, I suppose I own the copyright!**"

In 2009 Julian made contact with Lucy O'Donnell, who by then was Mrs Lucy Vodden:

"**I tracked Lucy down through my PA Annie Fowler (who is friends with Lucy's sister, Fran O'Donnell) when I heard that she was suffering from the incurable auto-immune illness lupus, but not long after in September 2009 she lost her battle with the disease. At around the same time I was working with the singer/songwriter James Scott Cook and he had written a song coincidentally called 'Lucy' about his grandmother who also, coincidentally, suffers from lupus. We decided to record it as a charity single for the two Lucys in our lives with a share of the proceeds going to the Lupus Foundation of America and, in the UK, to St Thomas' Lupus Trust. It was released via i-Tunes on December 15, 2009 and will remain on sale until we find a cure …**

"**It was my idea to use my Lucy drawing as the cover for the single; I thought it would be a nice touch.**"

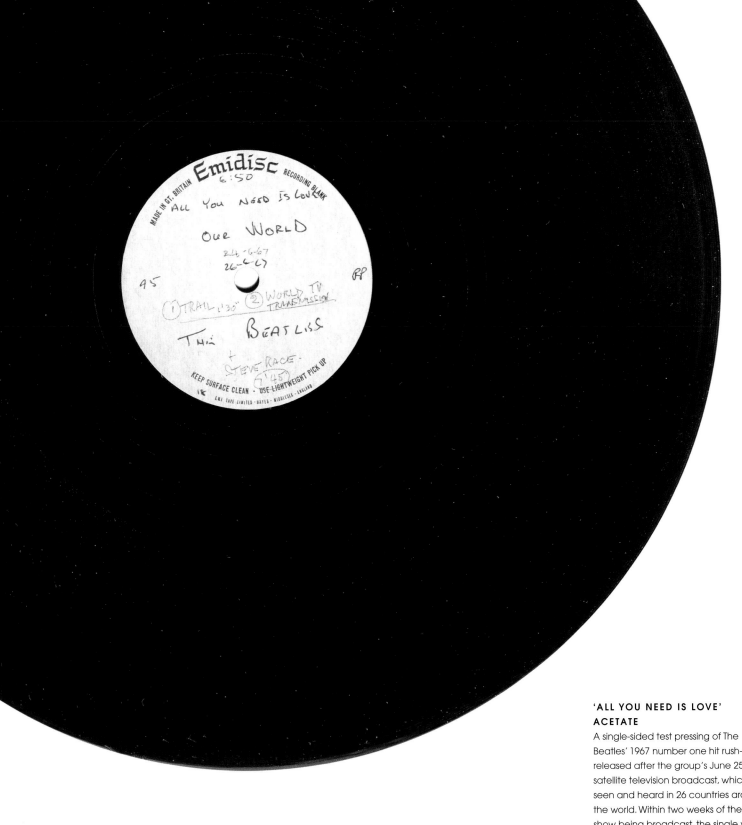

The handwritten label on the disc reads:

Emidisc 6:50
MADE IN GT. BRITAIN · RECORDING BLANK

ALL YOU NEED IS LOVE
OUR WORLD
24-6-67
26-6-67
95   PP
① TRAIL 1'30"   ② WORLD TV TRANSMISSION
THE BEATLES
+ STEVE RACE
7'45
KEEP SURFACE CLEAN · USE LIGHTWEIGHT PICK UP
EMI TAPE LIMITED · HAYES · MIDDLESEX · ENGLAND

**'ALL YOU NEED IS LOVE'
ACETATE**

A single-sided test pressing of The Beatles' 1967 number one hit rush-released after the group's June 25 satellite television broadcast, which was seen and heard in 26 countries around the world. Within two weeks of the TV show being broadcast, the single was in the UK shops.

After the TV show, changes were made to the song and during the following day five complete remixes were done. The finished version would have been produced as an acetate for approval by the group and producer George Martin who, for the first time ever, was credited on a Beatles' single.

HEY JUDE GOLD ALBUM

When the Beatles' plans for an album entitled *Get Back* were abandoned in 1970, Capitol Records decided to once again collect together a number of tracks not previously issued on an album in America and release them as the album *Hey Jude*.

Originally called *The Beatles Again,* the ten-track *Hey Jude* album featured the number one hits 'Can't Buy Me Love', 'Paperback Writer' and 'Hey Jude' plus top ten hits 'Lady Madonna' and 'The Ballad of John And Yoko' alongside 'I Should Have Known Better', 'Rain', 'Revolution', 'Old Brown Shoe' and 'Don't Let Me Down.'

It peaked at number two in the US charts in March 1970 and featured as the album cover a shot from The Beatles' last-ever photo session taken at John's Tittenhurst Park home, Ascot, in August 1969.

'HEY JUDE' GOLD SINGLE

The Beatles returned the top of the US charts in September 1968 – nine months after their last chart topper – with 'Hey Jude' which racked up sales of over 4.7 million copies worldwide in just two months.

Released on August 26, 1968, on both sides of the Atlantic, the record was both the first release on the group's new Apple label and The Beatles' longest-ever single at 7 minutes and 11 seconds.

George Martin was among those who believed singles could not run for that long but when he made his views known, he was "shouted down by the boys", with John asking, "Why not?" The Beatles' producer adds, "I couldn't think of an answer, really – except the

pathetic one that disc jockeys wouldn't play it. He (John) said, 'They will if it's us'."

The single hit the US chart at an all-time high of number 10 and went on to hold the number one spot for nine weeks, while in Britain it was the biggest-selling record of 1968 and also the group's 15th number one. It remains The Beatles' second most successful single ever with sales of over 10 million – just behind 'I Want To Hold Your Hand' with 12 million.

Reviewing the single in *Melody Maker* in August 1968, Keith Emerson, keyboard player with Nice and ELP, wrote, "It's nice to see the Beatles are also recording something that lasts for seven minutes, it gives you the chance to get into

what they are doing" while the paper's regular singles reviewer Chris Welch added, "'It's not staggering but it could grow on you' was the first reaction around pop land to seven minutes of fresh Beatlery."

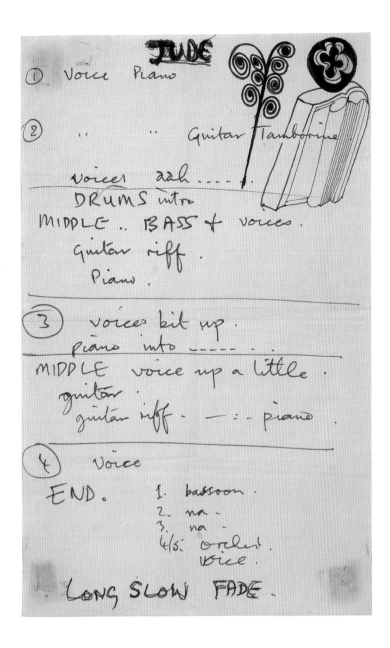

'HEY JUDE' RECORDING NOTES

When Paul was composing the song he wrote for Julian after the split between John and Cynthia, he broke down how he thought it should be structured into four sections, where he identified the instruments and voices.

Talking to *Rolling Stone Magazine*, Paul explained how the song had come to him as he was driving to see Cynthia. "I think it was just after John and she had broken up and I was quite mates with Julian. He's a nice kid, Julian. And I was going out in me car, just vaguely singing this song, and it was like, 'Hey Jules'. I don't know why, 'Hey Jules' – it was just this thing. 'Don't make it bad/ Take a sad song ...' And then I just thought a better name was Jude."

As Julian was only five when his parents split up and when Paul wrote 'Hey Jude', it's perhaps not surprizing to hear Cynthia say, "Funny enough, Julian didn't know about it for years and years and years, and then when he realized that 'Hey Jude' was about him, he felt really humbled."

Julian has strong feelings about the song Paul wrote for him:

"I can't pinpoint exactly when it was that I realized that 'Hey Jude' was written about me or for me, about what was going on at the time of Mum and Dad's break-up and how I must remain strong and together.

It would have been around the time when I was 10, 11 or 12. The funny thing is that Paul never talked to me about it specifically; in fact it was almost public knowledge before I heard about it. When I was about 20 or 21, I was on the promo TV circuit in America and Paul was on one of the same TV shows and our paths crossed, and that's when we first had a chance to talk and he laid it on the line there on the show.

"Hearing him say what it was about had a profound effect on me. In the beginning it was just something he wrote because he cared about me, and he cared about Mum and our situation, so who knew it would

turn out to be the beast that it is today and probably will be forever more ...

"I know it started out as 'Hey Jules' and I think it probably would still have worked, had he left it as 'Hey Jules'.

"I didn't get the recording notes from Paul, they were from an auction. It's curious because I would have thought that Paul might have wanted to buy them. Maybe when you're in the position they were in, you just don't remember to keep all the stuff you write and use."

GURU DEVA BRACELETS

These bracelets were worn by John during and after his trip to India in February 1968 to visit and study with the Maharishi Mahesh Yogi at his International Academy of Meditation in Riskikeshi, where Guru Deva was one of the teachers.

During the visit, John, his wife Cynthia and the other Beatles plus their partners were given the mantra 'jai guru dev om' to use in their daily meditations and John later used it in the song 'Across the Universe' which appeared on The Beatles' *Let It Be* album.

The Beatles first met the Maharishi in Bangor, North Wales on August 25, 1967, two days before their long-time manager Brian Epstein was found dead at his London home.

Later, disillusioned with the Maharishi, John would say, "We believe in meditation, but not the Maharishi and his scene. But that's a personal mistake we made in public," before adding, "I don't know what level he's on but we had a nice holiday in India and came back rested to play businessmen."

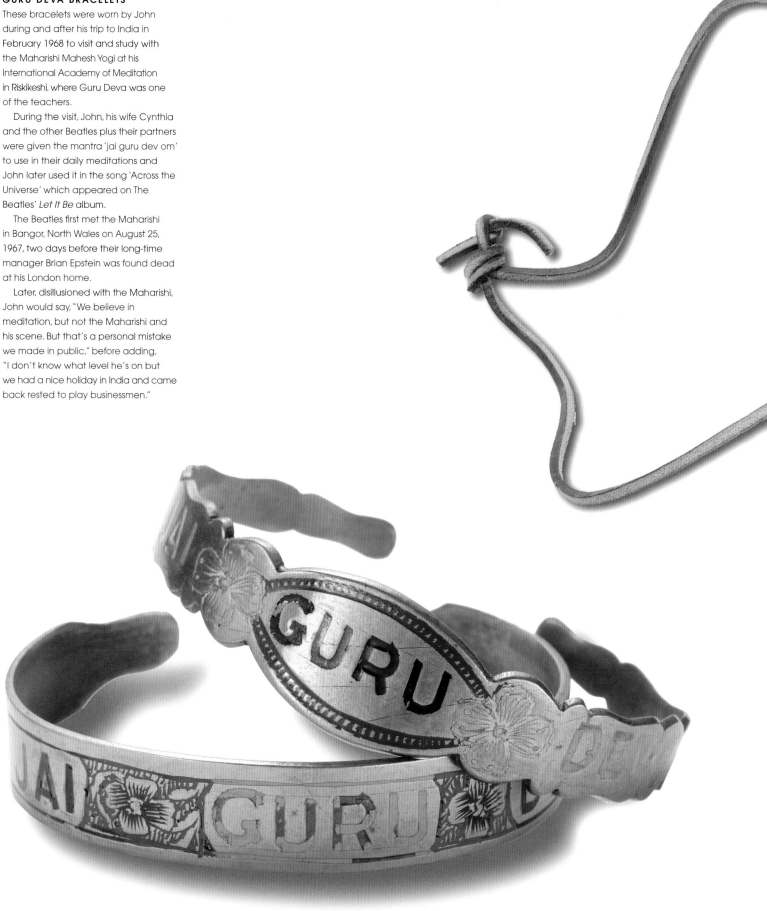

This Egyptian Ankh was worn by John in the late 1960s, a time when he had developed a deep interest in spiritual matters. It is the symbol of eternal life and translates from early hieroglyphics as the 'key of life'. John visited Egypt just once and while there said, "It's fantastic. It's amazing. I've been here before."

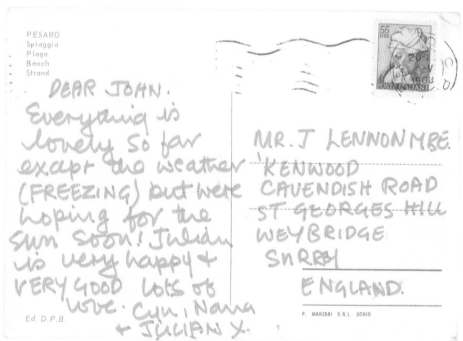

PESARO
Spiaggia
Plage
Beach
Strand

DEAR JOHN.
Everything is
lovely so far
except the weather
(FREEZING) but were
hoping for the
sun soon! Julian
is very happy &
VERY GOOD lots of
love. Cyn, Nana
+ JULIAN X.

Ed. D.P.B

MR. J LENNON MBE.
`KENWOOD
CAVENDISH ROAD
ST GEORGES HILL
WEYBRIDGE
SURREY
ENGLAND.

P. MARZARI S.R.L. SCHIO

1968 POSTCARD FROM CYNTHIA

During a holiday in Italy in 1968 with
son Julian and 'Nana' – her mother Lilian
– Cynthia sent this postcard from Pesaro
on Italy's Adriatic coast to John, who
was at home at Kenwood in Weybridge.
She included alongside his name the
letters MBE to signify the award The
Beatles received in 1965, and which
John returned in 1969.

PESARO
Giardini Pubblici
Jardins Publics
Public Avenue Quay
Öffentlichen Anlagen

LOVE
FROM
JULIAN
TO DADDY.
XXXX

MR J. LENNON.
'KENWOOD'
CAVENDSH ROAD
ST GEORGES HILL
WEYBRIDGE
SURREY ENGLAND.

Ed. D.P.B.

P. MARZARI S.R.L. SCHIO

1968 POSTCARD FROM JULIAN
From the same holiday, Julian penned
the words 'love from Julian' on his
postcard to his father with a picture
of Pesaro's public gardens.

"It's an absolute ha
someone not only
about you, but es
and especially ur
circumstances."

hour to have
write a song
ecially Paul,
der those

YER BLUES.

Yes I'm lonely wanna die
Yes I'm lonely wanna die
If I ain't dead already
Ooh girl you know the reason why.

In the morning wanna die
In the evening wanna die
If I'm dead already
Ooh girl you know the reason why.

a int

My mother was of the earth
My father was of the sky
But I am of the universe
And that's the reason why
Wanna die,
Wanna die
If I'm dead already
Ooh girl you know the reason why.

ain't

The eagle picks my eyes
The worm he eats my bones
I feel so   *'suicidal .*
Just like Dylan's Mr. Jones
Wanna die, Wanna die
If I ain't dead already
You know the reason why.

Black cloud cross my mind
Blue mist round my soul
Feel so suicidal
Even hate my Rock and Roll
Wanna die, Wanna die
If I ain't already
You know the reason why.

dead .

While studying and meditating with the Maharishi in India, in early 1968, John found time to write these lyrics to his song 'Yer Blues', which appeared on the 1968 album *The Beatles*, known as the *White* album.

John recalled that while in India he wrote some of his best songs but also added, "I was writing the most miserable songs on earth. In 'Yer Blues', when I wrote, 'I'm so lonely I want to die', I'm not kidding. That's how I felt. Up there trying to reach God and feeling suicidal."

It was one of over 20 songs written during The Beatles' trip to India which were then demoed in the studio at George's house before being taken into Abbey Road and completed in just two days in August 1968.

The song was a cheeky dig at the British blues born in late 1960s, which was led by the likes of Chicken Shack, Ten Years After and Fleetwood Mac. John told *Rolling Stone* that The Beatles were, "Super self-conscious people about the parody of Americans which we do and have done. Yes, there was self-consciousness about singing blues."

Reviewing *The Beatles* album, *Melody Maker* picked out 'Yer Blues' and pronounced, "Lennon takes over on a big funky rock 'n' roll number in slow tempo that has an Electric Flag feeling in parts. Then he goes into an imitation Elvis Presley 'Heartbreak Hotel' break, singing, 'I feel so suicidal, even hate my rock and roll'."

It was a song that John performed live on December 11, 1968 at The Rolling Stones' famous *Rock 'n' Roll Circus*, which was filmed under the direction of Michael Lindsay-Hogg in a circus big top with Mick Jagger as the ringmaster and assorted members of Fossett's Circus. The event, which cost £50,000, was shot in front of a live audience but has still never been broadcast.

As part of a bill that featured The Stones, The Who, Jethro Tull, Marianne Faithfull and bluesman Taj Mahal, John joined forces with Eric Clapton, Rolling Stone Keith Richards and Mitch Mitchell, drummer with Jimi Hendrix, in a super group called Dirty Mac to perform 'Yer Blues' for the first and only time on a British stage.

Five-year-old Julian was also at the party alongside Yoko Ono, who stood stage side during the performance.

APPLE CORPS WATCH

A souvenir promotional watch from the company that The Beatles launched in May 1967 as the successor to their original Beatles Ltd. business. It emerged as Apple Corps Limited in January 1968, with offices on London's Wigmore Street, although the original Apple company – Apple Music publishing – was started in May 1967.

Apple was launched with the now-famous Granny Smith apple logo which nobody has ever been credited with creating, although the name is said by some to have come from The Beatles' desire to make business fun and use a simple name based on children's rhyme, 'A is for Apple', while Paul once quipped, "It's a pun – apple core – see?"

At the time the Apple company was formed it involved all four Beatles plus NEMS directors Robert Stigwood (manager of the Bee Gees and Eric Clapton) and music agent and ex-band leader Vic Lewis overseeing The Beatles' affairs after the death in August 1967 of Brian Epstein, who had been around when the first Apple Music business was established.

Apple came about as The Beatles attempted to offset some of the top rate income tax they were paying, estimated to be around £3 million, and advizers suggested they invest in businesses related to their own work. Through Apple, they went into fashion, music publishing, records and films. The famous Apple boutique opened in London's Baker Street in December 1967 – with a glitzy party attended by John and George – and closed seven months later with a massive giveaway sale of stock worth £10,000.

Apple ran in a chaotic state for a few years and the group spent thousands of pounds on the various Apple enterprizes with Apple Records emerging as probably the most successful operation, thanks to artists such as Mary Hopkin, James Taylor, Billy Preston and Badfinger.

The company logo – a complete Granny Smith apple – was used for A-sides of records while an apple sliced in half was put on the B-sides, and from 1968 until 1975 all Beatles' group and solo recordings appeared on Apple, even though the band and the individuals were all still signed to EMI.

Paul once explained, "That's why Apple went wrong, because we didn't have the business sense", and Lennon confirmed things were not working out when he said, "I think it's a bit messy and it wants tightening up. We haven't got half the money people think we have … but we can't let Apple go on like this."

There were even plans – led by John – for an Apple School, where Julian Lennon, Zak Starkey and the children of Apple staff would be educated. A total of 20 children would be able to attend and *Magical Mystery Tour* actor Ivor Cutler was hired as a consultant while Ivan Vaughan, who had introduced John and Paul in Liverpool in the 1950s and gone on to become a teacher, was hired to be head teacher, but as the various Apple businesses struggled, the school plan fell apart.

Paul applied to dissolve both the legal partnership Beatles & Co (and the group) in 1970 and it was finally legally wound up in 1975, but each of the Beatles remained as directors of Apple Corps, which continues to look after the group's affairs, the catalogue of recordings plus image and merchandizing rights.

YELLOW SUBMARINE
FRAMED CELLS AND SKETCHES

A selection of original pictures of the characters and scenes from The Beatles' film *Yellow Submarine*, in which the fictitious and peaceful Pepperland is attacked by the anti-music group, the Blue Meanies.

After Old Fred, the conductor of *Sgt. Pepper's Lonely Hearts Club Band*, recruits the cartoon Beatles, they all set off in the Yellow Submarine and travel through the Sea of Time, Nowhere and the Sea of Holes to reach Pepperland for a final confrontation with the Blue Meanies.

The full-length cartoon – which involved 40 animators and artists, who produced over half a million cells – came from a series of Beatles' cartoon

films broadcast on American television in 1965. They were made by New York writer and producer Al Brodax, who persuaded Beatles' manager Brian Epstein to agree to the feature film and for the group to supply some new songs for the cartoon.

But according to John it was a way of fulfilling the group's contract with United Artists: "It was the third movie that we owed United Artists. Brian had set it up and we had nothing to do with it. But I liked the movie; the artwork."

The final script included contributions from The Scaffold's Roger McGough (who was apparently paid but uncredited) alongside the official writing team of Brodax, Lee Minoff, John Mendelsohn

and Eric Segal, while producer Brodax hired Canadian animator George Dunning as the director.

The film featured the voices of comedy actors Dick Emery and Lance Percival alongside John Clive (as John), Geoff Hughes (Paul), Peter Batten (George) and Paul Angelis (Ringo) and the respected *Halliwell's Film Guide* says of *Yellow Submarine*: "Way-out cartoon influenced by Beatlemania and the swinging sixties; hard to watch for non-addicts."

TB 17J

Reg to B.G.

D-903   INF2   Sc 35   27 J

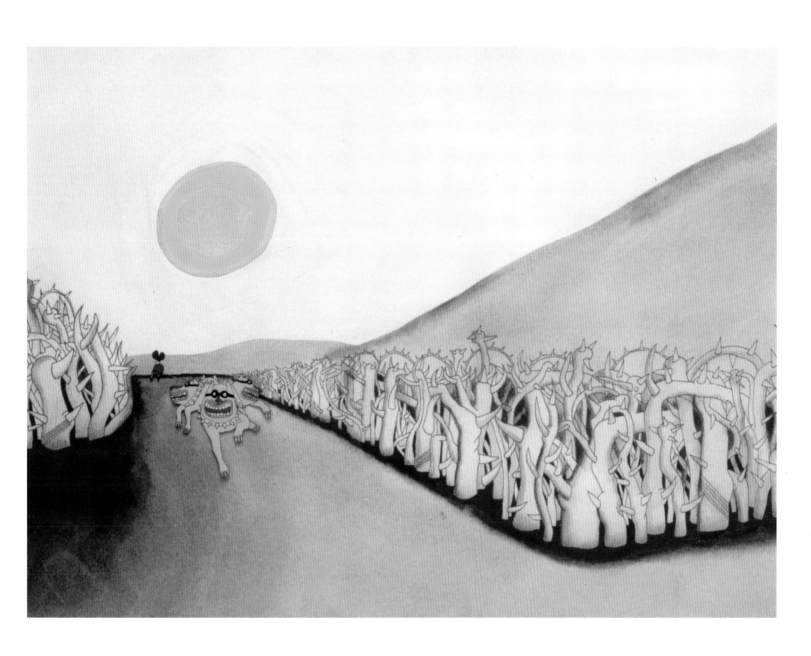

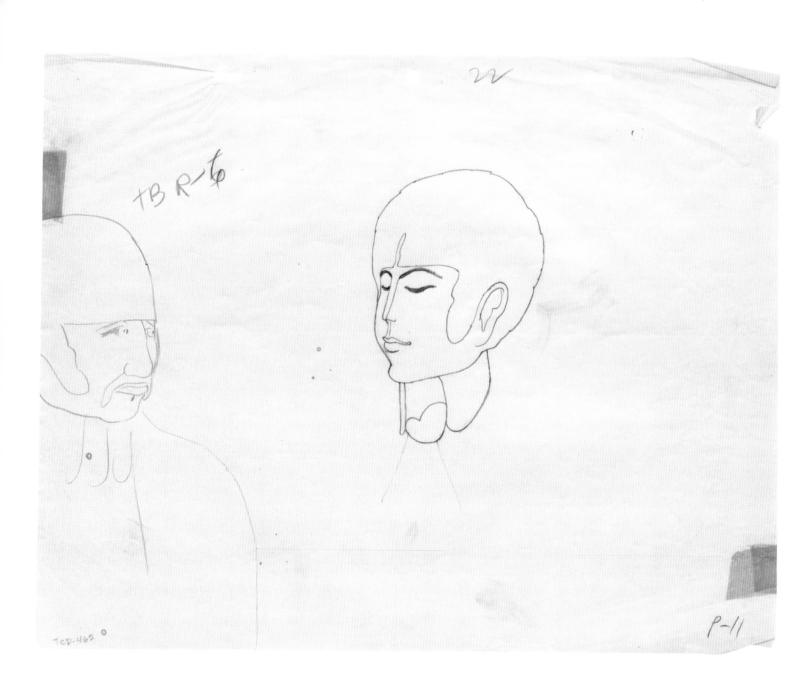

Yellow Submarine premièred at the London Pavilion in July 1968, where The Beatles were joined by musicians Donovan, Sandie Shaw, P.J. Proby, Mick Jagger and Alan Price, plus model Twiggy and disc jockeys Simon Dee and Tony Blackburn. Renowned film critic Alexander Walker wrote: " *Yellow Submarine* is the key film of the Beatles. It's a trip through the contemporary mythology that the quartet from Merseyside has helped to create."

However, themovie was never put on general release in the UK due to an assumption by the distributors that the film had been playing to small attendances at the London Pavilion during its initial run. Later, though, the box-office receipts showed that it had, in fact, been playing to capacity audiences and taking £7,000 a week, but Rank only put it in one third of their 200+ cinemas.

It opened in America in the autumn of 1968 and was a major box-office hit, playing to full houses across the country, and in 1999 a renovated and remixed version of *Yellow Submarine* was issued on video cassette and DVD.

WHITE ALBUM
GOLD ALBUM

Issued in November 1968, *The Beatles* was the group's first and only double album and thanks to its distinctive plain white sleeve with the group's name embossed on the front, it became known as the *White Album*.

It topped the US album chart from December 1968 for a total of nine weeks and was number one in the UK for a total of seven weeks and became the group's ninth consecutive number-one album in both America and Britain – and for John it was a better album than its world renowned predecessor *Sgt. Pepper*. "The Pepper myth is bigger but the music on the *White Album* is far superior," he once said.

The album, the first released on the group's Apple label, featured 30 songs, including four by George (who invited Eric Clapton to play on 'While My Guitar Gently Weeps') and 'Don't Pass Me By'

– the first song written by Ringo and recorded by The Beatles.

According to Alan Walsh, writing in *Melody Maker* in 1968, the album, "illustrates that the four members can each have their own direction under the artistic umbrella of the Beatles; pulling in different directions but never catapulting into anarchy."

'LADY MADONNA' GOLD SINGLE

Paul's song 'Lady Madonna' was released in the US and UK in March 1968 and was the last Beatles single to be issued on the Parlophone label in Britain and on Capitol in America. It was also the first single by the group to feature a song by George when 'The Inner Light', which he first recorded in India in January 1968, was issued as the B-side.

'Lady Madonna' was produced in Abbey Road in sessions on February 3 and February 6, 1968 and rush-released five weeks later after The Beatles had flown to India. Despite selling over a million copies in one week, the single peaked at number four in the US, although it reached number one in the UK with initial sales of 250,000.

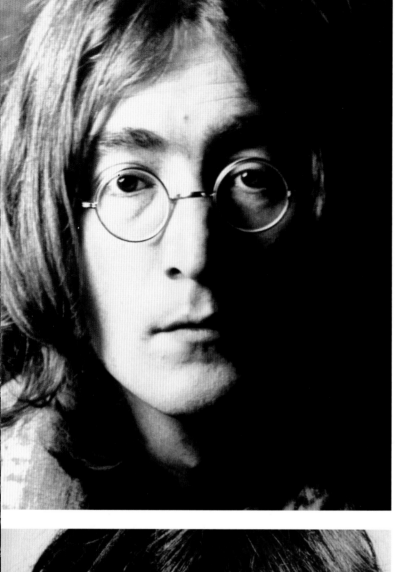

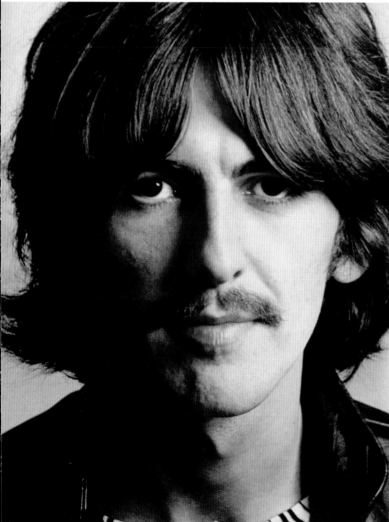
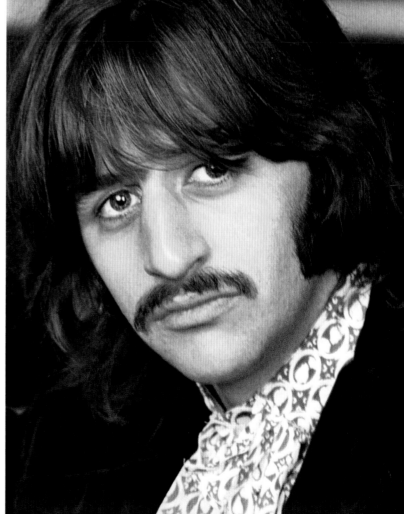

5

TOMORROW
NEVER KNOWS

AS THE CURTAIN BEGAN TO COME DOWN ON THE EXTRAORDINARY LIFE AND TIMES OF THE BEATLES – A DECADE OF UNPARALLELED SUCCESS, ADULATION AND OCCASIONAL RANCOUR PLAYED OUT UNDER THE CONSTANT GAZE OF THE PUBLIC – JOHN, PAUL, GEORGE AND RINGO ALL FACED NEW CHALLENGES, EACH ONE, AS A MUSICIAN AND BUSINESSMAN, A GROUP MEMBER AND AN INDIVIDUAL, FOCUSED ON AN EXCITING NEW FUTURE.

ABBEY ROAD   THE BEATLES

STEREO   SO-383
Side 1

1. COME TOGETHER BMI 4:16
(Lennon-McCartney)
2. SOMETHING BMI 2:59 (George Harrison)
3. MAXWELL'S SILVER HAMMER BMI 3:24
(Lennon-McCartney)
4. OH! DARLING BMI 3:26
(Lennon-McCartney)
5. OCTOPUS'S GARDEN BMI 2:49
(Richard Starkey)
6. I WANT YOU (She's So Heavy)
BMI 7:49 (Lennon-McCartney)
Produced by George Martin
Recorded in England
Manufactured by Apple Records

PRESENTED TO

THE BEATLES

TO COMMEMORATE THE SALE OF MORE THAN

ONE MILLION DOLLARS WORTH OF THE

APPLE RECORDS

LONG-PLAYING RECORD ALBUM

"ABBEY ROAD"

RIAA

CERTIFIED SALES AWARD

ABBEY ROAD GOLD ALBUM

Abbey Road was the last album The Beatles recorded together but it wasn't the last studio album to be released by the group. Work began on the album in February 1969 and ran through until August when all four Beatles made what was to be the last-ever visit to Abbey Road Studios by the whole group on August 20 for a final mixing and running order session. They had been recording in EMI's studios in London's St John's Wood district since their first demo session with Pete Best on June 6, 1962.

Issued in September 1969, it held the number one spot in America for 11 weeks, topped the British chart for 17 weeks and sold over four million copies worldwide in two months, although John described it simply as "a competent album."

The world-famous photograph for the front cover of Abbey Road was taken on the pedestrian crossing outside Abbey Road Studios, in London's St John's Wood, by Iain Macmillan on August 1969 ahead of the afternoon session to record 'The End', 'I Want You (She's So Heavy)' and 'Oh Darling'.

He was given just ten minutes to capture the right image during which time he took six shots while perched up a stepladder in the middle of the road as a helpful policeman held up the traffic. However, *Abbey Road* was not the original idea for the album's title as the band considered calling it *Everest* – engineer Geoff Emerick always smoked Everest menthol cigarettes. "We never really liked that but we couldn't think of anything else," recounts Paul. "Then one day I said, 'I've got it – Abbey Road.' It's the studio we're in and it sounds a bit like a monastery."

YELLOW SUBMARINE
GOLD ALBUM

First seen by The Beatles as a means of satisfying their contractual obligation to make three films for United Artists, *Yellow Submarine* became the group's third soundtrack album even though they only came up with four new songs for the cartoon film project.

John wrote 'Hey Bulldog' specifically for the film, while 'All Together Now' and 'It's All Too Much', along with George's 'Only A Northern Song', had all been considered for the *Sgt. Pepper* album. The title track supplied Ringo with his only A-side vocal credit in 1966 when it was released as a single coupled with 'Eleanor Rigby'.

The soundtrack album featured six instrumental pieces composed by George Martin and performed by his orchestra. It peaked at number two in the US and at number three in the UK in February 1969. Bizarrely, the sleeve notes for the *Yellow Submarine* album were in fact a review of The Beatles *White Album* written by Tony Palmer, published in the *Observer* and solicited by The Beatles' press agent Derek Taylor.

LEFT //
GEORGE HARRISON

This poster was included in George's American chart-topping *All Things Must Pass* triple album box set. It was taken at his Friars Park home in Henley-on-Thames by photographer Barry Feinstein, who worked with design partner Tom Wilkes on many of George's solo albums.

GEORGE HARRISON GUITAR POSTER

For this poster George was photographed on stage at New York's Madison Square Garden in August 1971 during his famous Concert For Bangla Desh charity concert. It was organized to aid victims of famine and war, and eventually raised over $13 million, thanks to the US top four and UK number one album *Concert For Bangla Desh*, released in January 1972, which featured the likes of Bob Dylan, Eric Clapton, Ringo Starr, Leon Russell, Billy Preston and Ravi Shankar.

'SOMETHING'
GOLD SINGLE

This song has a place in Beatles' history as the first track not written by John and Paul to be released as a single. George's track from the *Abbey Road* album was released as a double A-side with 'Come Together' and they topped the US charts in November 1969.

Described by John as "about the best track on the album", Something represented a breakthrough for George in songwriting terms as he was in constant competition with Paul and John, who later admitted, "Paul and I really carved up the empire between us because we were the singers. Paul and I did all the singing, all the writing. George never wrote a song till much later."

When 'Something' became the group's 18th American number one it put the quartet from Liverpool ahead of Elvis Presley in the list of US chart toppers, while in the UK the record stalled at number four,
the lowest place for a Beatles' single since their debut release 'Love Me Do' in October 1962.

'GET BACK'
GOLD SINGLE

'Get Back' became the only Beatles' single to feature the name of another artist on the label when Billy Preston was credited for his keyboard contribution to the record, which was famously performed and recorded on the roof of the group's Saville Row offices in January 30, 1969 – an event billed as the last-ever 'live' performance by The Beatles.

It was number one in America for five weeks, topped the UK chart and also became The Beatles' 17th US chart topper in five years and their 16th in Britain in six years despite the fact that the single was never "finished" according to John: "We were doing this rehearsal for a show which we never finished, so we got fed up and put the rehearsal out. There's chatting and messing about and all sorts on it."

Reviewer Derek Johnson was impressed as he concluded, "There's nothing adventurous or experimental about this track, just honest to goodness pop-rock, stamped with the unmistakeable hallmark of the masters."

GRUNDIG TAPE RECORDER

This 1960s' tape recorder was manufactured by the German consumer electronics company Grundig, which started business in 1945.

The Beatles used less sophisticated Grundig machines to tape some of their earliest performances in and around Liverpool as The Quarrymen, the Silver Beetles and The Beatles.

This portable TK140 four-track machine was located in John's attic recording studio at his Kenwood home and may have been installed by Apple Electronics "guru" (Mad) Alex Mardas who created studios and acquired recording equipment for The Beatles.

'INSTANT KARMA' GOLD DISC // OPPOSITE

The Beatles were still officially together as a group when John issued Instant Karma as his third "solo" single in February 1970.

Produced by Phil Spector, it was credited to John Ono Lennon with the Plastic Ono Band, although George played guitar and John's manager Allen Klein was among the backing vocalists. It peaked at number three in America and reached the top five in the UK.

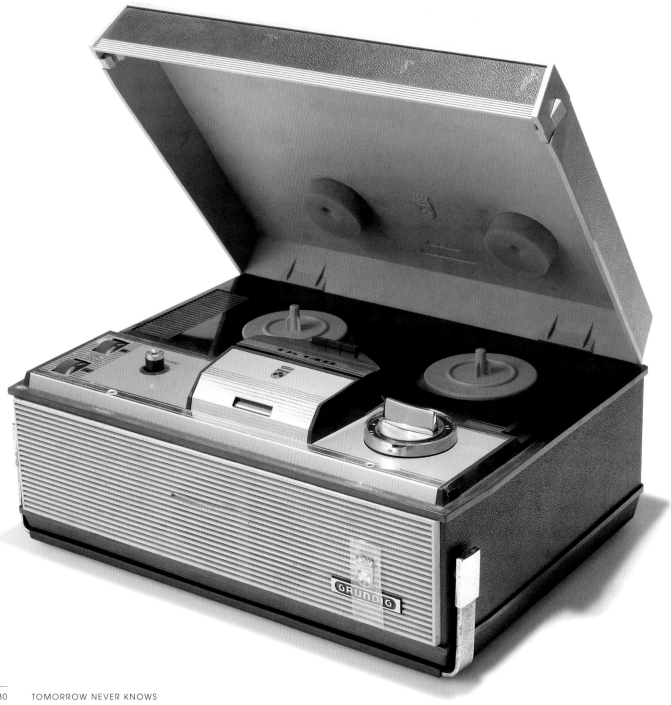

INSTANT
KARMA
(We All
Shine On)
(Lennon)

PLAY STEREO

Maclen
Music, Inc.
BMI–3 18

1818
(SAS-X43 1271)
Produced by
PHIL SPECTOR

Recorded In
England

LOUD
JOHN ONO LENNON

PRESENTED TO
JOHN ONO LENNON
TO COMMEMORATE THE SALE OF MORE THAN
ONE MILLION COPIES OF THE
APPLE RECORDS
POP SINGLE RECORD
"INSTANT KARMA"

CERTIFIED
RIAA
SALES AWARD

get copy of Heath's speech at the U.N. in N.Y. just after he came to power and went to see Nixon. the speech was about the internal struggle at home, lift each country to concentrate on their own underground!

New York • California • Orient • Round the World

JOHN'S NOTE RE HEATH SPEECH

Edward Heath came to power as Britain's Prime Minister in June 1970 when the Conservatives defeated Harold Wilson's Labour Party.

Months later he went to New York to deliver a speech to the United Nations assembly on October 23, 1970 and also paid a visit to US President Richard Nixon. John's note about the UK's new PM was written in America after he flew from London to New York on August 13, 1970. He never set foot on British soil again and within two years Britain was disrupted by a miner's strike. This was followed by another strike in 1974, which led to the notorious "three-day week" and effectively ended Heath's government.

HONDA MONKEY BIKE

Despite his notoriously poor eyesight and bad driving, John was a big fan of the small Honda Monkey motorbike and used it regularly around his Weybridge garden – and also at the Tittenhurst Park estate in Ascot when Ringo owned it – with Julian as a regular passenger.

The bikes were developed in the early 1960s by the Japanese Honda company and the first models, which had a small 50cc engine, were known as a Z100. They cost £67 at the time but original versions can now fetch up to £12,000 at auction.

Julian has great memories of riding on the bike with his dad:

"**I remember Dad riding it in the driveway in Weybridge with me as the passenger, and also riding it when we went to visit Ringo. I think I was allowed to sit up front and hold the handlebars but never to actually control it. It was a pokey little thing, you just don't think those little things could move that fast. It was great fun.**

"**I'm not sure why it's called a monkey bike, maybe because of the way the handlebars were shaped!?!**

"**I never took Dad as a dirt biker although he was a lad without a doubt, with the leathers and DA, but I never saw him as that outdoorsy type. My own love of motorcycles certainly goes back to those days.**"

'There were 99 acres of fields in which to be an idiot with him . . .' Eight-year-old Julian holds on during a rare visit to see his father at Tittenhurst Park, Ascot, 1971

Julian on riding the Monkey bike with John:

"One of those rare
got to spend time
these are some of
memories of us to

moments when I
with Dad …
my happiest
gether.."

BAG PRODUCTION MEMO
TO STAFF

Bag Productions was created in 1968 by John and Yoko to develop their film, music and art projects with arts critic Anthony Fawcett as their adviser. It was based in a ground floor office at Apple's Savile Row headquarters and dealt with all PR/media requests involving John and Yoko.

This note highlights some of the people who they considered important – radio disc jockey John Peel, Apple's chief radio plugger and fellow Liverpudlian Tony Bramwell, Jack Oliver, the head of Apple Records, and CBS Records.

When John returned his MBE in November 1969, he wrote to the Queen on Bag Productions notepaper and under his signature he described himself as "John Lennon of Bag". He also sent letters to the Prime Minister and the Secretary of the Central Chancery. In all three he explained that he was returning his MBE, "in protest against Britain's involvement in the Nigerian-Biafran thing, against our support of America in Vietnam and against Cold Turkey slipping down the charts."

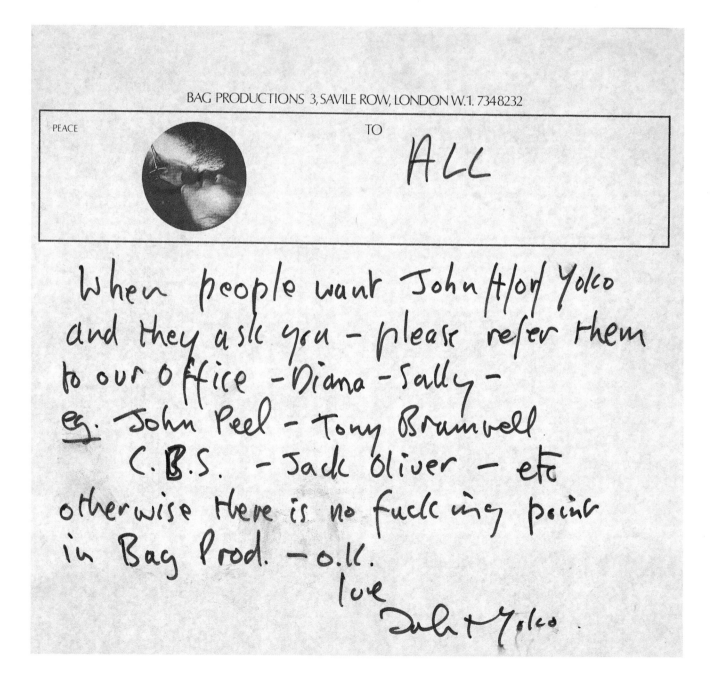

BAG PRODUCTIONS 3, SAVILE ROW, LONDON W.1. 734 8232

PEACE   TO   ALL

When people want John /t/or/ Yoko and they ask you – please refer them to our office – Diana – Sally – eg. John Peel – Tony Bramwell. C.B.S. – Jack Oliver – etc otherwise there is no fucking point in Bag Prod. – o.k.

love
John + Yoko.

'THE BALLAD OF JOHN AND YOKO' GOLD SINGLE

Released in May 1969, 'The Ballad Of John And Yoko' featured only John and Paul as George and Ringo were unavailable for the April 1969 recording session in Abbey Road Studios.

However, the absence of two Beatles didn't have any great impact on John during the recording of his song:" I don't regard it as a separate record scene ... it's the Beatles' next single, simple as that. It doesn't mean anything, it just so happened that there were only two of us there."

It peaked at number eight in America, where radio stations reacted to the use of the word "Christ" by bleeping it out or by flipping the record and instead playing George's track 'Old Brown Shoe'. In the UK it stands as The Beatles' last-ever number one single.

LET IT BE GOLD ALBUM

Let It Be has gone down in history as the last-ever official Beatles' release before the band finally split although it was actually recorded prior to the *Abbey Road* album.

The recording began in The Beatles' own Apple studios in Savile Row in January 1969 with the group planning an album titled 'Get Back' but by the time they had finished in May it was called *Let It Be*.

Even then, however, the album wasn't finished as legendary and controversial producer Phil Spector arrived on the scene in March 1970 to record, re-record and remix tracks for the re-named project.

The man who invented the "Wall of Sound" and recorded hits for The Ronettes, The Righteous Brothers and Ike & Tina Turner was something of a surprise choice to step into George Martin's shoes and the work he did on Paul's song 'The Long And Winding Road', which was done without the composer's consent or knowledge, went some way toward finally breaking up The Beatles.

John was a huge fan of Spector's work and was keen to get him involved with The Beatles, but even he was aware of his reputation. "The least you could call him is eccentric – and that's coming from somebody who's barmy."

The album was released in May 1970 with record US advance orders totalling over $3.7 million, was number one in America for four weeks and brought to an end an incredible run of 19 top-three albums in America in just over six years. It also topped the British chart for three weeks, bringing the Beatles their 11th UK top three album between 1963 and 1970.

'LET IT BE' GOLD SINGLE

The last official Beatles' single in the UK was released in May 1970 and climbed to number two in the charts, while in America it entered the charts at number six to set a new record for the highest new entry of all time.

George Martin's production of Paul's song began in January 1969 and finished nearly 12 months later, on January 4, 1970, when The Beatles – minus John who was on holiday – actually recorded for the last time as a band in Abbey Road.

J.L. collage.

To Julian, love Paul x.

COLLAGE

A distinct and original collage of
faces and bodies dedicated to
Julian from Paul. It was created by John
and given to Paul.

POCKET WATCH & STAND

The pocket watch and stand which
stood on John's bedside table at his
Kenwood home in Weybridge. It dates
from the 1960s and the watch, which
boasts a 15-jewel movement, fits into
an Oriental-style brass stand.

It was bought for John by Cynthia's
mother Lilian, who apparently was
often asked by John to, "Buy me books
bound in leather – and of course clocks.
It doesn't matter what's in them or if
they work. As long as they look good,
never mind the cost."

PRESENTED TO

JOHN ONO LENNON

TO COMMEMORATE THE SALE OF MORE THAN

ONE MILLION DOLLARS WORTH OF THE

APPLE RECORDS

LONG-PLAYING RECORD ALBUM

"IMAGINE"

CERTIFIED RIAA SALES AWARD

IMAGINE GOLD ALBUM

John's first solo number one album came out in October 1971, seven months after the official break-up of The Beatles.

It was recorded at John's home studio in his Tittenhurst Park mansion and credited to John Lennon and the Plastic Ono Band, which included the likes of George Harrison, Klaus Voorman on bass, drummer Jim Keltner and pianist Nicky Hopkins with Phil Spector as producer. Yoko Ono photographed and designed the album cover.

It hit the top spot in America for one week, was Britain's number one for two weeks and was the third US number one album by a solo Beatle after Paul's album *Ram* and George's *All Things Must Pass*, but according to *Melody Maker* writer Roy Hollingsworth, there was no real competition: "Lennon's won, hands down. If this were a new name it would be deemed the gutsy answer to the feeble state of rock."

The album's world-famous title track, which was written by John on the back of a hotel bill during a plane trip, was never released as a single in the UK but reached number three in the US charts in November 1970 behind Isaac Hayes' number one 'Theme from Shaft' and Cher's 'Gypsys, Tramps and Thieves'.

The album also included the track 'How Do You Sleep?', which was seen as a very poorly disguised criticism of Paul's writing, which John seemed to compare to "muzak". A *Rolling Stone* writer said of the song: "While I find it horrifying and indefensible, it nevertheless has an immediacy which makes it more compelling than most of the rest of the album."

For his part Paul simply observed: "I think it's silly. He says the only thing I wrote was 'Yesterday' and he knows that's wrong," while John later admitted, "I suppose I was a bit hard on him but that was how I felt at the time when I recorded it."

APPLE CAR MASCOT

When John decided to visit Scotland with Yoko Ono and her daughter Kyoko in July 1969 he invited Julian on the trip. And rather than travel in his chauffeur-driven Rolls-Royce, John decided to drive himself in a rather more modest Austin Maxi, which carried this Apple mascot on the bonnet.

The trip to the Scottish Highlands was to visit Durness and the home of his Aunt Mater which John had helped his uncle Bert renovate as a 15-year-old back in 1956. However John, who was a notoriously bad and irregular driver with very poor eyesight, lost control and the car veered into a ditch close to the town of Golspie.

All four passengers – John, Yoko, Kyoko and Julian – were taken to Lawson Memorial Hospital, where John had 17 stitches in a face wound, Yoko needed 14 stitches and injured her back and Kyoko had four stitches in a wound. Julian, who was staying with John and had been taken on the trip to Scotland without his mother's knowledge, escaped unhurt.

When she found about the accident, Cynthia Lennon took the first plane to Scotland and collected her son from Aunt Mater's home.

In 2002 a memorial stone commemorating John's links with Durness was unveiled in Scotland while Yoko apparently had the Maxi car returned to their Ascot home and mounted in the garden on a concrete plinth as she considered it "a happening."

Julian's lucky escape gives the car mascot special meaning:

"It is very significant to me. Firstly because Dad was not the best driver in the world because he couldn't see very well and secondly because when we had the accident I was the only one who was not injured or knocked out, no cuts or bruises. I remember telling Mum when she came to collect me from the hospital that I had seen my grandfather in the back of the car saying, 'You'll be OK, don't worry.' And I described to her my grandfather – Mum's father, Charles – who I'd never met.

"Again the car mascot represents another time and another place with Dad, anything I could get really, and that's why I had wanted to go to Scotland with him in the first place, plus we did have family there."

I'LL BE ON MY WAY

AFTER EIGHT YEARS TOGETHER AS THE BIGGEST BAND IN THE WORLD, THE FOUR YOUNG MEN WHO EMERGED FROM LIVERPOOL IN 1962 GRADUALLY SOUGHT FRESH OUTLETS FOR THEIR CREATIVITY AND NEW INTERESTS IN THEIR PERSONAL LIVES. BUT SOLO ALBUMS PLUS INDIVIDUAL PERFORMANCES AND PROJECTS WERE CONSTANTLY COUPLED WITH A SEEMINGLY NEVERENDING PUBLIC FASCINATION AND LOVE FOR THE MUSIC THEY CREATED TOGETHER ... AS THE BEATLES.

GIBSON LES PAUL GUITAR

Julian was given this guitar by his father – complete with its inscribed plate – as a Christmas present in 1973 when he was ten years old.

Gibson began making the Les Paul Junior in 1954 and continued with the original version until 1963 although there were changes in the shape, colour and pick-up. It was introduced as an affordable Les Paul electric guitar for aspiring young musicians and cost $120 when launched.

New York guitar repairman and stringed instrument maker Ron De Marino has a memory from the early 1970s of "helping John find a Les Paul Junior for his son Julian."

It was a guitar that Julian played, but always kept safe:

"I'd just started to learn to play the guitar at school, encouraged by our PE teacher, Brian Wynne. We started on borrowed acoustic guitars at school and we actually put on a show at Christmas. A whole bunch of us, including Justin Clayton, my oldest and best friend in the world, put a band together and did some classics – 'Roll Over Beethoven' and that kind of stuff with perhaps one or two original pieces thrown in.

"At Christmas time I remember Dad sent me one of the first kinds of Sony Walkman and I remember that when we did the performance at school I'd asked someone to put it on the side and press record. I decided to send the tapes to Dad and he heard it and obviously he wanted me to follow through because that is when I got the 1973 guitar. I thought that's it, this is what I want to do now …

"I learned how to play electric on this guitar initially. I never used it on stage – it was too precious to me, it wasn't even allowed to leave the house – I never used it on record, but I probably wrote a few tunes on it. In my eyes it was, and still is, the most beautiful guitar.

"The name Les Paul did mean something to me, even at that time. The rock 'n' roll school PE teacher Mr Wynne had greased-back hair and a DA, and talked about all of that stuff, so we had a little understanding."

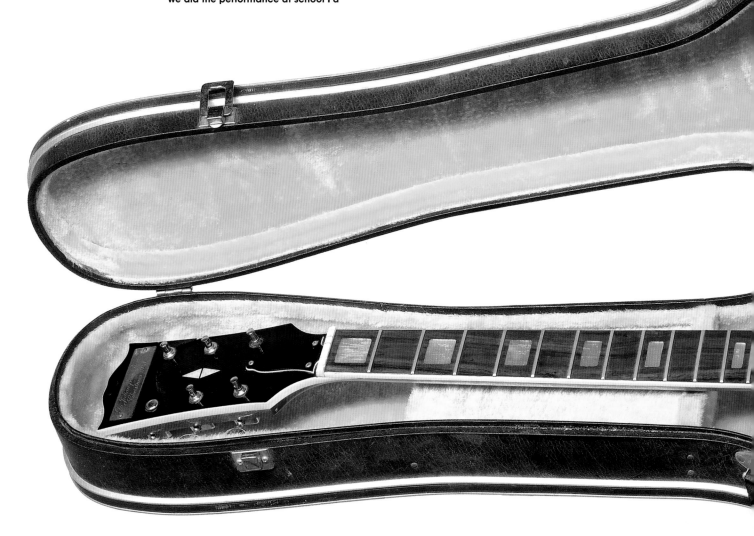

MIND GAMES GOLD ALBUM

When issued in November 1973, *Mind Games* was the first album to be released by John in over 12 months. It was also the first to be credited to just John Lennon, although tracks were later listed under the name John Lennon and the Plastic U.F.Ono Band, which included the likes of drummer Jim Keltner, guitarist David Spinozza, Gordon Edwards on bass and pedal steel virtuoso Sneaky Pete.

John's fourth post-Beatles album was issued in the midst of his fight against deportation from America and on the eve of his 18-month separation from Yoko – which became known as "the long weekend."

Recorded at New York's Record Plant studio and produced by John, the album hit the US top ten but peaked at number 13 in the UK.

MIND GAMES POSTER

A poster advertising John's 1973 solo album *Mind Games*, which saw him return to the US album top 40 chart for the first time in over two years.

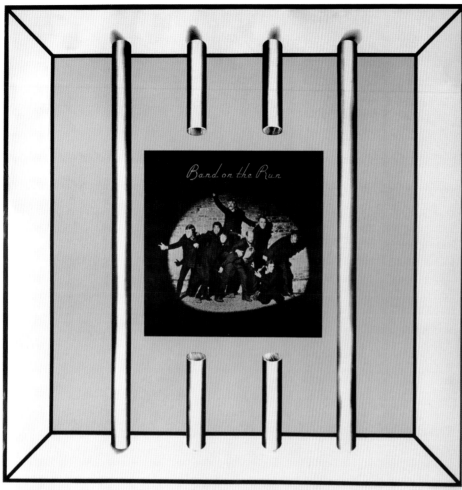

Band on the Run

is
Paul McCartney and Wings
NEW LP OUT NOW

PAS 10007
Marketed by EMI Records

BAND ON THE RUN POSTER

A poster reproducing the famous cover of the Paul McCartney and Wings album *Band On the Run* from December 1973, which featured the band – Paul, Linda McCartney and Denny Laine – alongside broadcaster Michael Parkinson, singer Kenny Lynch, American actor James Coburn, chef, broadcaster and MP Clement Freud, British actor Christopher Lee and boxer John Conteh.

Recorded in former Cream drummer Ginger Baker's studio in Lagos, Nigeria – where Paul and Linda were robbed at knifepoint – the album topped the charts in both the US and the UK, and featured the hit singles 'Helen Wheels', 'Jet' and the title track, which topped the charts in America. The album collected the Grammy for Best Pop Vocal by a duo or group.

Rolling Stone writer John Landau said that the album, which was written and produced by Paul, was "the finest record yet released by one of the four musicians who were once called the Beatles."

RED ROSE SPEEDWAY POSTER

The first album credited to Paul McCartney and Wings was in fact Paul's fourth album since leaving The Beatles. Recorded in London and Los Angeles, where Paul, Linda and Laine were joined by guitarist Henry McCullough and drummer Denny Seiwell, the album was produced by Paul and Linda but featured as engineer Alan Parsons, who had worked on The Beatles' *Let It Be* album and would later create The Alan Parsons Project.

Released in 1973, the album became Paul's second American number one – after his debut solo offering three years earlier – and also included his second solo US chart topping single 'My Love'.

OVERLEAF //

BEATLES 62–66 GOLD ALBUM
BEATLES 67–70 GOLD ALBUM

Released in April 1973, the albums known universally as "the red" & "the blue" were two double compilations which collected together The Beatles' recordings in their first five years and their final four years together.

The Beatles 1962–1966 (red) ran from 'Love Me Do' in 1962 to 'Yellow Submarine' in1966, with a further 24 tracks composed by John and Paul, produced by George Martin. It contained a total of 15 American and British number one singles and reached number three in both the US and UK in May 1973.

The Beatles 1967–1970 began with 'Strawberry Fields' in 1967 and ended with 'The Long And Winding Road' from 1970, plus another 21 tracks written by John and Paul, four songs from George and one composed by Ringo, with Phil Spector credited as producer on two tracks. With a total of 11 US and UK number one hit singles, the album reached number two in Britain but topped the US charts – the Beatles' 15th number one album – for one week in May 1973 before being replaced by Paul's *Red Rose Speedway* album, which in turn was succeeded by George's *Living In The Material World*.

The two albums featured photographs by Angus McBean. The "red" album cover was a shot from his original session for the 1963 album *Please Please Me*, which was taken on the first-floor landing of EMI's London headquarters in Manchester Square, while the "blue" cover was a later "identical" shot of The Beatles in the same location, taken in May 1969 for use on the abandoned *Get Back* album.

The wooden railing John, Paul, George and Ringo leant on for both the "old" and "new" shots was saved when the EMI building was demolished in the mid-1990s and placed in EMI Records' offices in Hammersmith, then moved to EMI's corporate headquarters in Kensington.

THE BEATLES 1962 – 1966

© 1973 Apple Records, Inc.
SKBO 3403
Side One

1. LOVE ME DO
   (Lennon & McCartney) BMI
2. PLEASE PLEASE ME
   (Lennon & McCartney) BMI
3. FROM ME TO YOU
   (Lennon & McCartney) BMI
4. SHE LOVES YOU
   (Lennon & McCartney) BMI
5. I WANT TO HOLD YOUR HAND
   (Lennon & McCartney) BMI
6. ALL MY LOVING
   (Lennon & McCartney) BMI
7. CAN'T BUY ME LOVE
   (Lennon & McCartney) BMI

PRESENTED TO
THE BEATLES
TO COMMEMORATE THE SALE OF MORE THAN
ONE MILLION DOLLARS WORTH OF THE
APPLE RECORDS
LONG-PLAYING RECORD ALBUM
"THE BEATLES 1962-1966"

CERTIFIED
RIAA
SALES AWARD

PRESENTED TO

THE BEATLES

TO COMMEMORATE THE SALE OF MORE THAN

ONE MILLION DOLLARS WORTH OF THE

APPLE RECORDS

LONG-PLAYING RECORD ALBUM

"THE BEATLES 1966-1970"

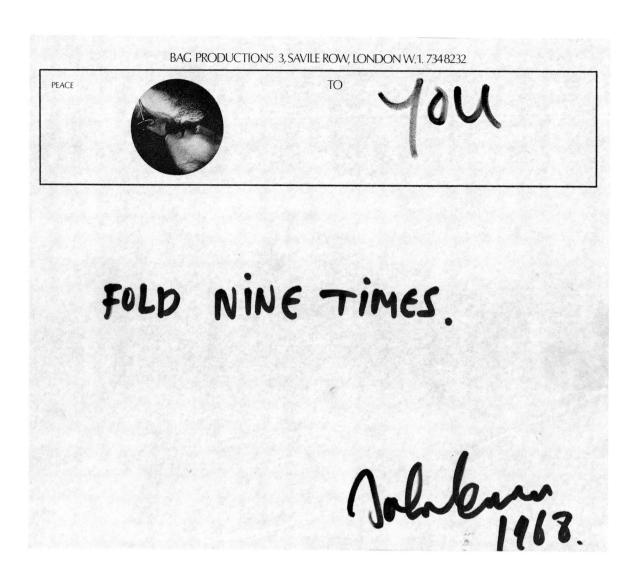

MEMO BY JOHN

The words "fold nine times" were written on Bag Production notepaper by John in 1968 and addressed to "You".

It seems the instructions to fold the paper that many times were in answer to the proverbial question as to whether a piece of paper could actually be folded nine times. It can't – and certainly a piece of Bag Productions notepaper would be too small anyway – but people at America's Stanford University have claimed that it is possible.

Using the name Bag for their company developed from "bagism" which was created by John and Yoko, and involved wearing a bag over the whole body in protest at prejudice based on appearance and in order to further awareness of their various causes.

Speaking to David Frost on British television in June 1969, when he and Yoko appeared on the broadcaster's top-rated show, John answered the question "what is bagism?" with "It's like … a tag for what we all do, we're all in a bag and we realized that we came from two bags. I was in this pop bag, going round and round in my little clique, and she was in her little avant-garde clique, going round and round, and you're in your little tele-clique. And we all sort of come out and look at each other every now and then, but we don't communicate."

IMAGINE POSTCARD

With the relationship between John and Paul severely strained following the break-up of The Beatles, John's answer to Paul's *Ram* album cover was this notorious *Imagine* album postcard he sent to Julian at his home in North Wales – with a reminder of John's telephone number in New York.

Parodying Paul's pose, which saw him holding a sheep in a photo taken by Linda, John was pictured hanging onto a pig in a very public dig at his former songwriting partner and he then included the shot as a postcard, which was given away with his 1971 *Imagine* album.

The postcard sent to his son in 1971 had the added bonus of a personal message written around the edge of the front photograph, which read "Farmer J wrestling with an agricultural problem" plus the words "a pig" next to an arrow pointing to the beast in question.

Paul's *Ram* album came out in June 1971, just one month after John, George and Ringo, who all wanted Allen Klein to take over as manager of the group, finally confirmed through their counsel that they accepted Paul's decision to leave the group and would not appeal against the appointment of a receiver to look into the group's affairs.

Imagine appeared four months after that, although John would go on record to claim, "It was not a terrible, vicious, horrible vendetta."

For Julian the *Imagine* postcard was just a note from his dad:

"At the time I didn't relate to what the postcard was all about. Dad had moved away and contact with him was little and precious, and I just saw it as making contact and never looked at it any deeper to see what he might be suggesting or saying. I didn't attach any significance to it, it was a picture of my Dad with a pig … The thing is, it didn't seem that weird … it made total sense!

"I was never sure what I thought when I understood what it was all about. I was not going to take sides. It was a time and a place, and we all have our moments."

WALLS AND BRIDGES GOLD ALBUM

Recorded in New York in June and July 1974 at the Record Plant studios, *Walls And Bridges* featured Elton John, Nilsson, Jim Keltner, Klaus Voorman, Jesse Ed Davis ... and Julian Lennon as musicians.

Eleven-year-old Julian was taped playing drums during the recording of the track 'Ya Ya'. Years later he was quoted as saying at time, "Cor that's me and Dad'. It meant a lot."

The album was John's last-ever US number one album during his lifetime and it also included his first American solo chart-topping single 'Whatever Gets You Thru The Night', which featured Elton on keyboards and vocals. John's appearance in the US singles charts in December 1974 coincided with Paul, George and Ringo all having American chart hits at the same time.

While Elton was convinced the record would be a hit, John was less sure and the two musicians reached an agreement that if the song topped the charts, John would join Elton in concert. As good as his word, John duly appeared at New York's Madison Square Garden on Thanksgiving Night (November 28) in 1974, and joined Elton on versions of 'Whatever Gets You Thru The Night', 'Lucy In the Sky With Diamonds' and 'I Saw Her Standing There', which he had only ever sung with Paul: "It was a really strange experience singing an early Beatles song that I never really sang and singing it with somebody else. I was actually thinking,

'Oh, I wonder what Paul will think of this'."

The album, which reached number six in the UK in October 1974, featured as part of the cover artwork paintings done by John as an 11-year-old schoolboy, along with photographs of him taken in his New York penthouse apartment by renowned American photographer Bob Gruen, who also captured Julian sitting alone in the studio.

Even though he got to play on* Walls and Bridges, *Julian has mixed feelings about his time in New York:

"This photo was taken in New York at the Record Plant Studios. I'm sitting on the couch in front of the mixing desk looking lost and lonely while Dad just got on with whatever he was doing. Mum had come over with me, but she had then gone onto California to stay with drummer Jim Keltner and his wife. It was a very odd time and I got quite bored and would try to amuse myself.

"I didn't know I was on the album until I actually received a copy and when I played it through and heard that on the end I just went 'Hey, that's me'. And I had a credit too. On the back of the album it said, 'Starring Julian Lennon on drums and Dad on piano and vocals'. That was cool! Apparently I told Dad later that if I had known he was recording I would have played better!"

Julian on his playing dums on 'Ya Ya':

"So I just went out
and started bang
with one stick and
came in and start
They had the tape
was that. It was fur

nto the studio
ng on a snare
eventually dad
ed doing 'Ya Ya'.
rolling and that
while it lasted."

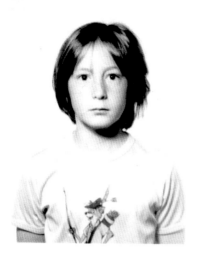

CERTIFIED COPY OF AN ENTRY OF BIRTH

REGISTRATION DISTRICT _Liverpool S_

_1963_ BIRTH in the Sub-district of _Sefton Park_

Columns:–	1	2	3	4	5	6
No.	When and where born	Name, if any	Sex–	Name and surname of father	Name, surname and maiden surname of mother	Occupation of father
	Eighth April 1963 14th Sefton General Hospital Sefton Park	John Charles Julian	Boy	John Winston LENNON	Cynthia LENNON formerly POWELL of 251 Menlove Avenue Liverpool	Musician (Guitar

CERTIFIED to be a true copy of an entry in the certified copy of a Register of Births in the District above
Given at the GENERAL REGISTER OFFICE, LONDON, under the Seal of the said Office, the

BXA 063807

This certificate is issued in pursuance of the Births and Deaths Registration Act 19
purporting to be sealed or stamped with the seal of the General Register Office
relates without any further or other proof of the entry, and no certified copy purpor
effect unless it is sealed or stamped as aforesaid.

CAUTION:– Any person who (1) falsifies any of the particulars on this certific
false, is liable to prosecution.

Form A502M (S.336335) Dd.151845 90,000 1/74 JC&SLtd

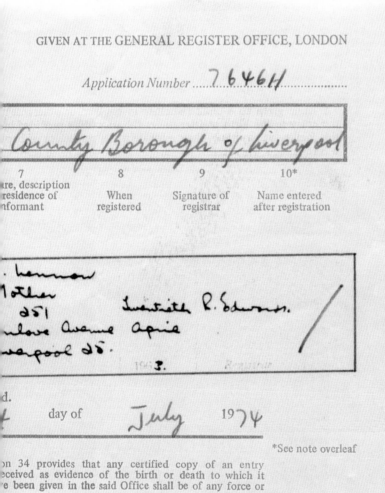

GIVEN AT THE GENERAL REGISTER OFFICE, LONDON

Application Number ......7 6 4 6 H

County Borough of Liverpool

7	8	9	10*
re, description residence of nformant	When registered	Signature of registrar	Name entered after registration

hennon
Mother
d51
enlove Avenue April
iverpool d5.

Twentieth R. Edwards.

d.
day of ___July___ 1974

*See note overleaf

on 34 provides that any certified copy of an entry
eceived as evidence of the birth or death to which it
e been given in the said Office shall be of any force or

uses a falsified certificate as true, knowing it to be

BIRTH CERTIFICATE

It was May Pang who engineered the reunion between John and Julian. May, With help from the Apple office in London, organised the necessary paperwork (including a copy of his birth certificate) for getting Julian over to see his father. This is the original copy of Julian's birth certificate which she obtained. On the certificate it describes John as a "musician (guitar)". The passport photo is the same as the one that appeared in Julian's passport. Julian is ten years old.

Julian recalls:

"The first trip I made to the USA to see Dad was just after Christmas 1973 when Mum and I flew to Los Angeles. That was followed by a second trip just a few months later. In July 1974 Mum and I made the voyage on the *SS France*. It was particularly memorable because Elton John and his band were on board! The well-known percussionist Ray Cooper was also a passenger and this proved to be an auspicious meeting because when I was 18 I went to stay with Ray in London. It was my first stay away from home and Ray tried to teach me to play drums and piano better, but I was 18, young and ready to have fun, and the idea of practising anything went out the window!"

SHAVED FISH

This poster was part of the campaign for John's 1975 compilation album *Shaved Fish,* which reached number 12 in the US and made the top ten in the UK.

It was a collection of the 11 hit singles released by John and the Plastic Ono Band between 1969 ('Give Peace A Chance') and 1975 ('#9 Dream'), which featured on his *Live Peace In Toronto, Imagine, Sometime in New York City, Mind Games* and *Walls And Bridges* albums.

The album was released just a month after John's deportation order was reversed and his son Sean was born. Its title was based on the name of a Japanese dish of fried fish.

POSTCARD TO JULIAN

This postcard was sent from Japan by John in 1977 when he was in Karuizawa – a popular mountain resort in the Nagano district – and includes a handy guide to the town's pronunciation ("Ka Ri Za") plus a local phone number and Yoko's "have a cool summer" message.

Julian says:

"I got this postcard from Dad when he, Yoko and Sean went to visit Yoko's family and spent the summer touring Japan and Hong Kong."

'FAME' GOLD SINGLE

In 1975 John visited David Bowie in the studio in Philadelphia during the making of his US and UK top ten album *Young Americans*.

The former Beatle helped out by playing guitar on Bowie's version of John's song 'Across The Universe' and also co-wrote the track 'Fame' with Bowie and guitarist Carlos Alomar before joining in on the backing vocals.

'Fame' became Bowie's first-ever number one single when it topped the US charts in September 1975, although it peaked at number 17 in the UK and was one of the few songs which John co-wrote with anybody other than Paul or Yoko.

BOWIE, YOKO AND JOHN
David Bowie, Yoko Ono and John Lennon
get together at the 17th annual Grammy
Awards in New York in February 1975
ahead of their collaboration on the
record 'Fame'.

GIBSON LES PAUL 25/50 GUITAR
Launched in 1978, this Gibson Les Paul guitar was a present from John to Julian. It was issued to commemorate the 25th anniversary of the Les Paul model guitar (although it was actually introduced in 1977) and also the 50th anniversary of guitarist Les Paul's career in the music business. Produced in tobacco sunburst, natural, wine red and black, they cost $1,200 in 1978.

For Julian the guitar was a welcome gift:

"Dad gave me this special order rare model guitar – it was always exciting to receive something like this from my dad.
    "When I visited Dad we would sit down together and he would teach me a few chords and help me improve my technique."

THE BEATLES AT THE HOLLYWOOD BOWL GOLD ALBUM

The Beatles played the world-famous Hollywood Bowl in Los Angeles three times and two of those concerts – albeit a year apart – were used to create the first and only Beatles official "live" album.

Their concert on August 23, 1964, in front of over 18,000 fans was taped by Capitol Records, who benefited from the introduction of some new equipment in The Beatles' line-up. According to a local newspaper the band had ordered "some powerful amplifiers – 100 watt" for the show, but according to producer George Martin, the end product still left a lot to be desired.

"It was like putting a microphone at the tail of a 747 jet. It was one continual screaming sound and it was very difficult to get a good recording," he said. When The Beatles returned to Los Angeles in 1965, they played two more concerts at the Hollywood Bowl on August 29 and August 30. Both shows were again taped by Capitol for possible release although the first of these was considered unusable due to a technical hitch.

In fact the recordings of both the 1964 and 1965 shows were turned down by both The Beatles and Capitol, and remained unseen and unheard for a further 12 years until May 1977 when *The Beatles At The Hollywood Bowl* was finally released.

Producer Martin and The Beatles' long-time engineer Geoff Emerick eventually managed to create an acceptable album combining six songs from the 1964 concert with seven songs from the August 30, 1965 concert to make a 13-track live album which reached number one in the UK and number two in the US, where it became only the second Beatles album to be certified platinum.

BADGE-MAKING MACHINE

John was an avid fan of badges (or buttons, as they are called in America), and wore them during the last years of The Beatles and throughout his time in New York, where they were often linked to the various political or humanitarian causes he supported.

Sometime in the early 1970, after he had moved to New York, John got hold of this badge-making machine and he created badges to promote his *Walls And Bridges* album, which said, "Listen To This Button" with a UK version which urged "Listen To This Badge".

Apparently he made hundreds of other buttons including this one of his own *Yellow Submarine* cartoon image, taken from the film's letterhead, which he gave to May Pang so that he would "always be with her".

During the Beatle years John sported badges which said "Exciting New Offer", "I Still Love The Beatles" and "You Are Here" and, later in America, he wore buttons with the messages "Elvis", "Indict Rockefeller" and "Not Insane" and – at Phil Spector's urging – one which said simply "Mono".

Julian recently obtained the badge machine from May Pang, who had kept it since the 1970s:

"When Dad and May Pang were together it was always a fun time, always a lovely time with no stress, no pressure, no darkness, no anger.

"May told me that Dad had seen the badge-maker in a magazine and got her to order it for him. He was always trying out different sorts of promotional tools and ideas. He did all kinds of promo stuff with stickers and badges – with 'Listen to this sticker' and 'Listen to this button'.

"I'd never seen a badge machine before. It was such a fun thing as a kid to make your own badges and it was really cool to walk around with whatever you wanted on your jacket. Dad and I had a great time making badges for ourselves and friends. The badge, "Hello My Name is Julian", is one I made for May.

"Badges were all part of Dad's protests and support for causes – it was very much the time when he had his cap and denim jacket covered in badges. I was amazed to discover that May has had it ever since and it still works!"

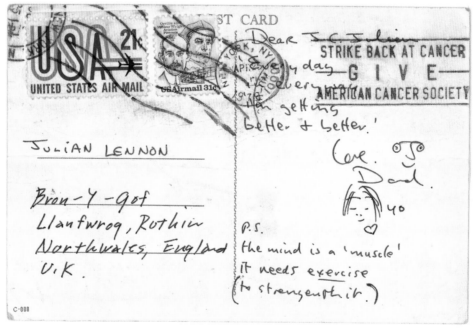

POSTCARD FROM JOHN TO JULIAN, 1979

John was an enthusiastic writer of postcards and this one was sent to Julian from New York in 1979. The J.C, J presumably refers to his son's three first names – John Charles Julian – and the phrase "Every day in every way I'm getting better and better" was a mantra-like suggestion created by French psychologist Émile Coué, who died in 1926. He was a pioneer of self-help and the force behind a form of conscious autosuggestion known simply as "couesim."

John usually signed his postcards with a cartoon of himself (with Yoko often adding a drawing of herself and a heart) and this one carried the added postscript "the mind is a muscle". John also used postcards to make observations and correct mistakes. He often wrote to *Melody Maker* in London to clarify points about issues involving both himself and The Beatles. On occasions he would add the P.S. "LP winner" as every week *MM* gave a record token to the best reader's letter.

For Julian postcards were a way of keeping in contact with his dad:

"I had to buy all of the postcards back … it's more than likely that when we moved house stuff got lost or somebody would steal something. It was good to get them back because they reminded me of certain times and places – so they are special to me – but it was crazy to have to buy them back! Postcards suited Dad because I think he would panic a bit about email today. He'd write something, send it and then regret it after he sent it. Email can be dangerous stuff!

I know, I've done that, been there!"

"'The Mind Is A Muscle' is a philosophy he lived by – if you don't keep your mind active and keep learning you won't grow. After he started signing the cards with his drawings of his face and glasses I'd create faces from my name and other words when I was signing and scribbling things. I received this postcard from dad after I spent my birthday with him on Long Island. It's the last time I saw him…"

XMAS CARD

With his album *Tripping The Live Fantastic* in both the US and UK charts and no live dates on the agenda, Paul busied himself with his Christmas card list in 1991 and sent this one to Julian.

As a well-publicised artist, it's likely that Paul also drew the front cover illustration as it is signed with a small PMc in the corner.

Julian says:

"I treasure Paul's friendship. We are still close and get together whenever we are in the same town at the same time! We keep in touch, especially at Christmas and birthday times."

14th April, 1997

Dear Julian,

Please find enclosed a white label vinyl advance copy of my new album "Flaming Pie".

Only 200 have been pressed and sent to "extremely groovy" people such as yourself. Linda and I hope it brings you a moment or two of joy. We also hope you *have* a record player - and if not, why not get one! Failing that, I understand that when warmed up it can be made into a rather attractive plant pot holder.

Love,

Paul

Paul McCartney

*I hope you'll enjoy this!
Best personal regards from me
and the family.*

xxx

love from linda ♡

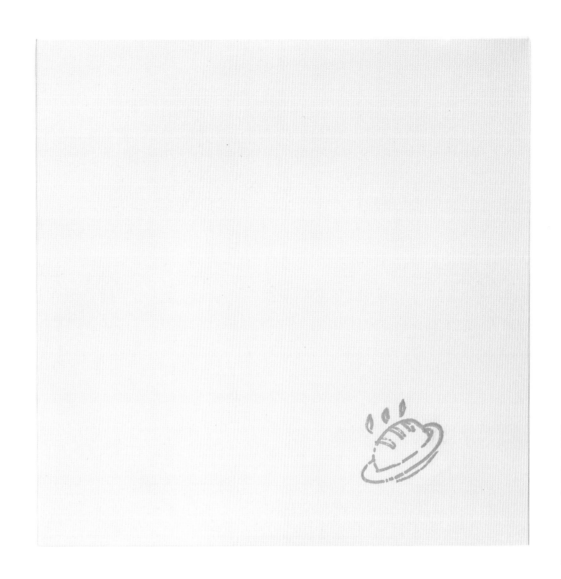

A month ahead of the release of his new album Paul sent just 200 "white label" vinyl advance copies of *Flaming Pie* to what he dubbed "extremely groovy" people – and Julian was one of them.

It arrived with a note dated April 14, 1997 and the personal handwritten message: "I hope you'll enjoy this! Best regards from me and the family."

FLAMING PIE

After they worked together on the *Beatles Anthology* series, Paul teamed up with his former Beatles producer George Martin and ELO's Jeff Lynne to produce *Flaming Pie,* his first new studio album for over four years,

Released in 1997, the *Flaming Pie* album reached number two in both the US and the UK and featured the hit singles 'Young Boy', 'The World Tonight' and 'Beautiful Night'. It was Paul's twenty-third album since 1970 and the breakup of The Beatles.

THE
WHITE FEATHER
FOUNDATION

Starting my own charity was something I'd been thinking about for a long time. I have always been plugged into humanitarian and environmental issues but I was keen to do more, so in 2008 I set up *The White Feather Foundation*, which promotes awareness and raises funds for these causes around the world.

Many people ask me how significant the name White Feather is. The answer is 'very'. One of the things my father said to me was that should he pass away, if there was some way of letting me know he was going to be ok, or that we were all going to be ok it was by presenting me with a white feather in some way, shape or form ... which is what happened to me when I was on tour in Australia promoting *Photograph Smile*. I was given a white feather by the elder of an Aboriginal tribe who asked me to help them because I had a voice that could be heard. I produced a documentary about them called *Whaledreamers*, which highlighted their struggle for survival and their connection and respect for Mother Earth. A white feather has since proved on numerous occasions to be very prevalent in my life ...

The name of my foundation is in memory of dad's words and what a white feather means to me – peace, spirituality and helping those in need.

Please check out the website for more information:

www.whitefeatherfoundation.com

Julian Lennon

The White Feather Foundation will benefit by receiving a share of the proceeds from the sale of this book.

OPPOSITE //
(Clockwise from top)
- Medicinal plant cultivation instruction, Yachaicurí School, Yurayaco community, Caquetá, Colombia.
- Indigenous woman of the Waurá, Xingu Indigenous Park.
- Public school of the rainforest village of Kwamalasamutu, southern Suriname.

BEATLES DISCOGRAPHY 1963–1996

ORIGINAL UK ALBUMS

22-03-63	Please Please Me
22-11-63	With The Beatles
10-06-64	A Hard Day's Night
04-12-64	Beatles For Sale
06-08-65	Help!
03-12-65	Rubber Soul
05-08-66	Revolver
01-06-67	Sgt Pepper's Lonely Hearts Club Band
22-11-68	The Beatles (The White Album)
17-01-69	Yellow Submarine
26-09-69	Abbey Road
08-05-70	Let It Be

OFFICIAL UK COMPILATION ALBUMS

09-12-66	A Collection of Beatles Oldies Parlophone Records
19-04-73	1962–1966 (The Red Album)
19-04-73	1967–1970 (The Blue Album)
19-11-76	Magical Mystery Tour
07-03-88	Past Masters, Volume One
07-03-88	Past Masters, Volume Two
15-11-88	The Beatles Box Set
30-11-94	Live at the BBC
21-11-95	Anthology 1
18-03-96	Anthology 2
28-10-96	Anthology 3
13-09-99	Yellow Submarine Songtrack
13-11-00	The Beatles 1
17-11-03	Let It Be… Naked
16-11-04	The Capitol Albums, Volume 1,
11-04-06	The Capitol Albums, Volume 2
20-11-06	Love

ORIGINAL UK SINGLES

05-10-62	Love Me Do / P.S. I Love You
11-01-63	Please Please Me / Ask Me Why
11-04-63	From Me To You / Thank You Girl
23-08-63	She Love You / I'll Get You
29-11-63	I Want To Hold Your hand / This Boy
20-03-64	Can't Buy me Love / You Can't Do That
10-07-64	A Hard Day's Night / Things We Said Today
27-11-64	I Feel Fine / She's a Woman
09-04-65	Ticket to Ride / Yes It Is
23-07-65	Help! / I'm Down
03-12-65	We Can Work It Out / Day Tripper
10-06-66	Paperback Writer / Rain
05-08-66	Yellow Submarine / Eleanor Rigby
17-02-67	Strawberry Fields Forever / Penny Lane
07-07-67	All You Need Is Love / Baby You're a Rich Man
24-11-67	Hello Goodbye / I Am the Walrus
15-03-68	Lady Madonna / The Inner Light
30-08-68	Hey Jude / Revolution
11-04-69	Get Back / Don't Let Me Down
30-05-69	The Ballad of John and Yoko / Old Brown Shoe
31-10-69	Something / Come Together
06-03-70	Let It Be / You Know My Name
20-03-95	Baby It's You / I'll Follow the Sun
	Devil in Her Heart / Boys
12-12-95	Free as a Bird / I Saw Her Standing There
	This Boy / Christmas Time
04-03-96	Real Love / Baby's in Black
	Yellow Submarine / Here, There and Everywhere

ORIGINAL UK EPS

12-07-63	Twist and Shout
06-09-63	The Beatles' Hits
01-11-63	The Beatles (No. 1)
07-02-64	All My Loving
19-06-64	Long Tall Sally
04-11-64	Extracts from the Film A Hard Day's Night
06-11-64	Extracts from the Album A Hard Day's Night 06-04-65 Beatles for Sale
04-06-65	Beatles for Sale (No. 2)
06-12-65	The Beatles' Million Sellers
04-03-66	Yesterday
08-07-66	Nowhere Man
08-12-67	Magical Mystery Tour

ORIGINAL US ALBUMS

10-01-64	Introducing… The Beatles
20-01-64	Meet the Beatles!
10-04-64	The Beatles' Second Album (US album)
26-06-64	A Hard Day's Night
20-07-64	Something New
15-12-64	Beatles '65
22-03-65	The Early Beatles
14-06-65	Beatles VI
13-08-65	Help!
06-12-65	Rubber Soul
16-07-66	Yesterday… and Today
08-08-66	Revolver
02-06-67	Sgt Pepper's Lonely Hearts Club Band
27-11-67	Magical Mystery Tour
25-11-68	The Beatles (The White Album)
13-01-69	Yellow Submarine
01-10-69	Abbey Road
26-02-70	Hey Jude
18-05-70	Let It Be

ORIGINAL US SINGLES

23-04-62	My Bonnie / The Saints
25-02-63	Please Please Me / From Me to You
27-05-63	From Me To You / Thank You Girl
16-09-63	She Loves You / I'll Get You
26-12-63	I Want To Hold Your Hand / I Saw Her Standing There
27-01-64	My Bonnie / The Saints
30-01-64	Please Please Me / From Me to You
08-02-64	All My Loving / This Boy
15-02-64	Roll Over Beethoven / Please Mister Postman
02-03-64	Twist and Shout / There's a Place
16-03-64	Can't Buy Me Love / You Can't Do That
23-03-64	Do You Want to Know a Secret / Thank You Girl
27-03-64	Why / Cry for a Shadow
27-04-64	Love Me Do / P.S. I Love You
21-05-64	Sie Liebt Dich / I'll Get You
01-06-64	Sweet Georgia Brown / Take Out Some Insurance On Me
06-07-64	Ain't She Sweet / Nobody's Child
13-07-64	A Hard Day's Night / I Should Have Known Better
20-07-64	I'll Cry Instead / Happy Just to Dance with You
20-07-64	And I Love Her / If I Fell
24-08-64	Matchbox / Slow Down
15-02-65	Eight Days a Week / Don't Want to Spoil the Party
19-07-65	Help! / I'm Down
13-09-65	Yesterday / Act Naturally
06-12-65	We Can Work it Out / Day Tripper
21-02-66	Nowhere Man / What Goes On
30-05-66	Paperback Writer / Rain
08-08-66	Yellow Submarine / Eleanor Rigby
13-02-67	Penny Lane / Strawberry Fields Forever
17-07-67	All You Need Is Love / Baby You're a Rich Man
27-11-67	Hello Goodbye / I Am the Walrus
18-03-68	Lady Madonna / The Inner Light
26-08-68	Hey Jude / Revolution
05-05-68	Get Back / Don't Let Me Down
04-06-69	The Ballad of John and Yoko / Old Brown Shoe
06-10-69	Come Together / Something
11-03-70	Let It Be / You Know My Name
11-05-70	The Long and Winding Road / For You Blue
31-05-76	Got to Get You into My Life / Helter Skelter
08-06-76	Ob-La-Di, Ob-La-Da / Julia
17-04-95	Baby It's You / I'll Follow the Sun Devil in Her Heart / Boys
12-12-95	Free as a Bird / Christmas Time
04-03-96	Real Love / Baby's in Black

JOHN LENNON DISCOGRAPHY
1968–2005

All the records were released under John Lennon's name except where noted. All the songs were written by John except where noted. Most of John's solo records were originally released on the Apple label. Reissues and CDs have generally been on EMI or Parlophone in the UK, Capitol in the US.

1. SINGLES

These were the only songs issued as singles in their own right, and written for that purpose rather than as album tracks. The A-sides can now be found on various compilation albums. 'Free As A Bird' and 'Real Love' appear on Volumes I and II, respectively, of The Beatles' *Anthology*.

(Plastic Ono Band)
Give Peace A Chance
UK: 4-7-1969
US: 7-7-1969
APPLE

(Plastic Ono Band)
Cold Turkey
UK: 24-10-1969
US: 20-10-1969
APPLE

Instant Karma!
UK: 6-2-1970
US: 20-2-1970
APPLE

'Power To The People
UK: 12-3-1971
US: 22-3-1971
APPLE

Happy Xmas (War Is Over)
UK: 24-11-1972
US: 1-12-1971
APPLE

2. ALBUMS

(John Lennon & Yoko Ono)
Unfinished Music No. 1 - Two Virgins
UK: 29-11-1968
US: 11-1-1968
APPLE/ TETRAGRAMMATON

(John Lennon & Yoko Ono)
Unfinished Music No. 2 – Life With The Lions
UK: 9-5-1969
US: 26-5-1969
APPLE

(John Lennon & Yoko Ono)
Wedding Album
'John And Yoko' 'Amsterdam'
UK: 7-11-1969
US: 20-10-1969
APPLE

(The Plastic Ono band)
Live Peace In Toronto
UK and US: 12-12-1969
APPLE

John Lennon/Plastic Ono Band
UK and US: 11-12-1970
APPLE

Imagine
UK: 8-10-1971
US: 9-9-1971
APPLE

(John & Yoko/Plastic Ono Band)
Some Time In New York City
UK: 15-9-1972
US: 12-6-1972
APPLE

Mind Games
UK: 16-11-1973
US: 2-11-1973
APPLE

Walls And Bridges
UK: 4-10-1974
US: 26-9-1974
APPLE

Rock'N'Roll
UK: 21-2-1975
US: 17-2-1975
APPLE

(John Lennon & Yoko Ono)
Double Fantasy
UK and US: 17-11-1980
GEFFEN

(John Lennon & Yoko Ono)
Milk And Honey
UK: 23-1-1984
US: 19-1-1984
POLYDOR

Live In New York City
UK and US: 24-1-1986
EMI (UK)/CAPITOL (US)

Menlove Ave
UK: 3-11-1986
US: 27-10-1986
PARLOPHONE (UK)/CAPITOL (US)

3. COMPILATIONS

Shaved Fish
UK and US: 24-10-1975
APPLE

Imagine: John Lennon
UK: 10-10-1988
US: 4-10-1988
PARLOPHONE (UK)/CAPITOL (US)

Lennon Legend
UK: 27-10-1997
US: 24-2-1998
PARLOPHONE (UK)/CAPITOL (US)

John Lennon Anthology
CD1 Ascot:
CD2 New York City
CD3 The Lost Weekend
CD4 Dakota
UK: 2-11-1998
US 3-11-1998
CAPITOL

Wonsaponatime
UK: 2-11-1998
US: 3-11-1998
CAPITOL

Acoustic
UK: 1-11- 2004
US: 2-11-2004
PARLOPHONE (UK)/CAPITOL (US)

Working Class Hero: The Definitive Lennon
UK: 3-10-2005
US: 4-10-2005
PARLOPHONE (UK)/CAPITOL (US)

VISUAL INDEX

Pages 2–3

13

16

17

18

18

19

20

21

23

25

28

29

30

31

31

32

33

33

34

34

36

37

38

39

39

40

41

41

41

45

46

47

48

48

49

51

54-55

55

56

57

58

58

59

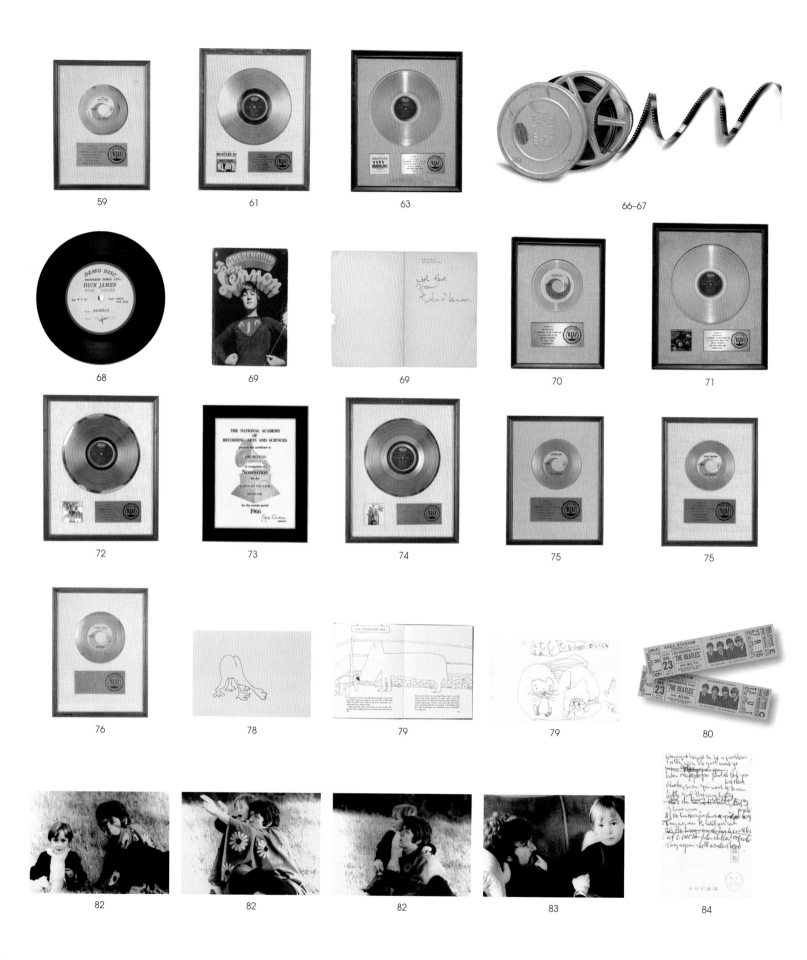

59

61

63

66–67

68

69

69

70

71

72

73

74

75

75

76

78

79

79

80

82

82

82

83

84

85

88

89

90

91

92

93

94

94–95

95

97

97

99

100

101

102

103

104

105

106

107

110

111

112

113

114

115

116

117

118

119

120

120

124

125

126

127

128

129

130

131

132

133

133

136

137

138

138

140

141

142

143

146–147

148

148

150

151

152

153

154

155

157

160

160–161

162

163

164

166

167

168

170–171

172

173

174

175

INDEX

AUTHOR'S ACKNOWLEDGEMENTS AND BIBLIOGRAPHY

Brian Southall would like to extend his grateful thanks to Julian Lennon – for his observations and his memories (and for lunch!) – and to John Cousins and Celia Quantrill and also to Roland Hall at Carlton. I would also like to acknowledge back issues of *Melody Maker* and *New Musical Express* as important sources of information alongside the following published works:

Beatles Anthology (Cassell & Co. 2000); *Beatles Encyclopedia* by Bill Harry (Virgin Publishing 2000); *Beatles Live!* By Mark Lewisohn (Pavilion Books 1986); *Complete Beatles Recording Sessions* by Mark Lewisohn (Hamlyn/EMI 1988); *Billboard Book of Number One Hits* by Fred Bronson (Billboard Publications 1997); *Billboard Book of Number One Albums* by Craig Rosen (Billboard Publications 1996); *In My Life: John Lennon Remembered* by Kevin Howlett & Mark Lewisohn (BBC Books 1990); *John Lennon: The Definitive Biography* by Ray Coleman (Pan Books 1995); Memories of John Lennon (Sutton Publishing 2005); *Paul McCartney: Many Years From Now* by Barry Miles (Vintage 1998); *Northern Songs* by Brian Southall (Omnibus 2007).

PICTURE CREDITS

BLOOD BROTHERS

Dad's legacy lives on in both of us.